Esther's Anointed Such Times

Touching the Scepter of God

ESTHER PERARA

First Edition

PAGE PUBLISHING, INC.
New York, NY

First originally published by Page Publishing, Inc. 2018

ISBN 978-1-64082-783-7 (Paperback)
ISBN 978-1-64082-784-4 (Digital)

Printed in the United States of America

To my many readers, many thanks!

In my life's journey of challenging but anointed spiritual scepter touchings, my Lord Jesus Christ hath never left nor forsaken me (Hebrews 13:5B); therefore, in revealing His book—writings for this Esther—for "such a time as this" (Esther 4:14), I have come to one conclusion—it all is just a setup!

Being used through it all for God's glory!

It's as if this lifetime sovereign ministry has a predestined great commission start in the possibility of going into all the world witnessing how I got over or came through heretofore and up to this point!

Fasting and praying surely to be able to continue trusting, "walking by faith and not by sight" (2 Corinthians 5:7), I'm able to say, "All is well, through all the hell!"

As I continue believing unselfishly for all of you, our Lord's willing Esther spirit's the same in Jesus's name!

To the love of my life, my late husband, United States Air Force Chief Master Sergeant Robert H. Perara Sr. (CMSgt, retired), who won the spiritual race that was set before him (1 Corinthians 7:14). I thank God for my Robert—for the life, the living, the loving, and the legacy.

To the loving sacrifice of my children—Keith, Kevin, Mary, Robert Jr., and Margaret—as well as other family and friends who have patiently supported me in my faithful endurances.

Contents

Introduction

If you have a heart to see people set free, you will be able to identify with this book. In the Bible, Esther's heart was hurting for her people, and she wanted to see them saved from the hands of Haman. We all know someone (family members, friends, acquaintances, etc.) who desires to live right for God. Christians love to see people freed from their bondages (bound by sin). We are responsible for duplicating the role that Mordecai possessed and encourage one another through our trials and tribulations.

In today's church age, we are in need of the heart of Esther for such a time as this. The harvest is ripe, and in my commitment to evangelism, I pray that you will be encouraged as I share my personal encounters of my life with you. I trust that you will be inspired as you see the hand of God moving in seemingly impossible situations. The true account of Esther is written for such a time as this to promote peace in your lives even during the midst of a storm (Haman spirit).

Furthermore, it is also my prayer that it will not take you forty years as it did for me to see the movement of God over my loved ones. The commitment to pursue patience was a critical element in my life. I prayed and waited on an answer from the Lord for my husband, Robert, to be saved before he departed from this earth. I also watched our children proclaim their salvation one by one. Lord, in my obedience, this modern-day spiritual Esther is determined to give You all the glory!

This book gives us a glimpse of how the biblical Esther's anointing intercedes, touches, and transforms lives (with the spiritual scepter extended) to release the favor of God on even your life and in your situations. It is among the most vital weapons available to us today as well as a reflection of *God's unconditional love and favor*. This anointing may pull you out of your comfort zone as you pray to God for peace for the lost and bound. John 3:16 gives us never-ending hope that everyone will have a chance at salvation through Christ, for all our spiritual "touching the scepter of God" needs!

Esther's love for her people represents the true church of the Living God, and through Christ Jesus (as the desired Glorious Church), they are saved, delivered, washed in the Word to become one in Christ (Matthew 16:18, 19; John 17:21; Ephesians 5:26, 27). Through Esther's life, we see that the "star" latched on to her name but especially now as a representation of Jesus Christ, the Son of the Living God. The Lord desires to shine from within each of us as we become a unified living church.

Chapter One

Opportunity Waits

It has been said that "opportunity knocks but once. However, a recent television commercial says, "Opportunity does not knock, but opportunity waits." Being I - Evangelist Esther E. Perara do normally think as a Biblical theologian, I hear the Lord reminding me of Hebrews 13:8: "Jesus Christ—the same yesterday, today, and forevermore." He *is* our opportunity. We must believe Hebrews 13:5, where God says, "I will never leave you nor forsake you."

We have all heard that Jesus stands at the door (of our hearts) and knocks,[1] waiting for any man to open and receive Him as Savior and Lord. Yet even after opening the door and letting Him in, our actions reveal that we somehow forget He will always love us. Jesus is seated at the right hand of God,[2] interceding for us until we believe we are spiritually seated in heavenly places with Christ Jesus.[3]

While walking through our seasons, the Esther anointing is ready for such a time as this. The anointing is the very presence of God strengthening us. It is God's plan and desire for the Holy Spirit to be in us and to empower us for every mission.

We thank God for His grace and mercy while He waits for us to walk in our purpose. I encourage you to take advantage of the opportunity today to serve Him. We need to serve the Lord while we wait for our predestined missions in our obedient opportune times. Also, we should always remember to walk in love. Hebrews 13:1 says, "Let brotherly love continue." *Continue* means to "be, stay, remain, nonstop" (obedience), which is something we must do. Now I am

1 Revelation 3:20–21.
2 Romans 8:26–27.
3 Ephesians 2:5–6.

not perfect by any means. I thank my Lord that He did not give up on me, which has taught me not to give up on others.

Historical Background

Esther, a beautiful Jewish orphan, was adopted by her cousin Mordecai who tenderly cared for her and raised her as his daughter. While Mordecai served in the palace of King Ahasuerus, Queen Vashti (the king's wife) declined an invitation to appear before him. A decree was issued to the palace, unaware of her nationality. Mordecai told Esther not to reveal her family background or nationality. Eventually, Esther was chosen as the new queen.

Sometime later, the king promoted a man name Haman to prime minister. Haman was second-in-command to the king and was very prideful. He ordered all the king's officials to bow down to him whenever he passed by, but Mordecai refused to bow. Haman was enraged because of Mordecai's disobedience, especially when he found out that Mordecai was a Jew (Esther 3:4–6). Therefore, Haman, having the king's favor, set in motion a plan to kill not only Mordecai but all the Jews.

As the historical episode unfolded, the state of chaotic affairs for the Jews was at hand with Haman's threat. But God and His unconditional love for all His beloved Jewish people prevented them from being destroyed.

Mordecai heard of the decree that was issued to have all the Jews killed. He was greatly distressed and dressed himself in sackcloth as he sat outside the gates of the palace. When Esther was told about Mordecai's actions, she sent her eunuch to find out what was wrong. Mordecai told the eunuch of his concerns in great detail and also instructed him to tell Esther to go before the king to beg for mercy and plead for her people. However, Esther sent word back stating that she could not go before the king as Mordecai requested because the king must first extend his gold scepter before anyone could appear before him. She added that the king had not sent for her in thirty days.

Upon receiving Esther's response, Mordecai replied:

> Do not think in your heart that you will escape the king's palace anymore than all the other Jews. For if you remain completely silent at this time, relief and deliverance will arise for the Jews from another place, but you and your father's house will perish. Yet who knows whether you have come to the kingdom for "such a time as this"? (Esther 4:13–14)

Mordecai's words of encouragement allowed Esther to overcome her concern to go before the king without being summoned. After she instructed to gather all the Jews to declare a fast, Esther made her history-making, sold-out vow, "I will go to the king, which is against the law; and if I perish, I perish!" (Esther 4:16).

Furthermore, Mordecai's encouraging words to Esther provides similarities to God's encouragement to Jesus as He faced the cross, while we hold dear the promise of John 3:16: "For God so loved the world, that He gave His only begotten Son, that whoever believes in Him should not perish, but have everlasting life."

It should curl our toes as we capture a mental picture of the ultimate price that Jesus visualized as He moved closer to Calvary.

> And He was withdrawn from them about a stone's throw, and He knelt down and prayed, saying, Father, if it is Your will, take this cup away from Me; nevertheless not My will, but Yours be done. (Luke 22:41–42)

Think of the amazing grace bestowed upon us and the thankfulness we should have for the sacrifice of our precious Lord and Savior Jesus Christ, Son of the loving God. Do you see Jesus's commitment to be used only for the glory of Father God? Because of the commitment of Christ, we received the blessed cancellation of our debts as He paid for all of our sins. He redeemed (bought us back) and reconciled us back to God. All I can say is, "Thank you, Jesus."

Jesus, who knew no sin, chose to accept His plight at Calvary. He submitted to the cross to redeem all those who believe in Him and for the desire for Christ to be seen in each of us. Esther also submitted to God's purpose and became an example for us.

We are not to take these privileged opportunities lightly, but we are to submit to God daily through our Lord Jesus Christ. Christians should always take heed to His purpose for us, never being selfish and ashamed of the gospel of Christ (Romans 1:16). We are to trust in abundant life what Christ has given us (John 10:10). It is the same abundant life that nullified Haman's selfish plan to destroy the Jews, God's chosen people.

At this point, the Lord says to all of us doubters that we have a right to ask Him about our situations and circumstances. "Lord, why me?" I recall Bishop T. D. Jakes's book *Why? Because You Are Anointed*, where he answered the question. He said it is "because of the Anointing," the very presence of the Holy Spirit's power within us when we receive Jesus as our Lord and Savior.

God promises in 1 Samuel 17:47, "The battle is the Lord's and He will give him the enemy into our hands." Remember Haman? He had the same evil spirit. So why should we worry? God gives us exactly what we need as we engage in spiritual warfare.[4] We trust our provisional God for all of His visions for us and remember to seek His kingdom first,[5] knowing that just as He provides for the sparrows, He will do the same for us.

In December 2006, my pastor's wife, Lady Doris Smith, so eloquently taught us in Sunday school that all our situations and circumstances are not about us, "not one bit." Esther's heart revealed that it was not about her, and she allowed God to truly use her. Although the word *God* was not mentioned anywhere in the book of Esther, the Spirit of Christ was revealed in the book and to all mankind throughout the Bible.

---

[4] 2 Corinthians 10:3–5.

[5] Matthew 6:33–34.

At the close of this chapter, you may have a desire to have the spirit of Esther. If you already acquired the heart of Esther in your life, can you be a witness and share it with others?

Chapter Two

Preparation Stage

Buckle up your seatbelts. You're about to experience the journey of some of the ups and downs in my life. The unconditional love of God has prepared the way for me to share my story that prayerfully will be a witness to you.

In the previous chapter, "Opportunity Waits," the Lord is waiting for us to come to Him. It takes me back to when it all began with referring to one of my early favorite scriptures, Psalms 31:15: "My times are in Thy hand." I'm reminded of my mother, the late Margaret Grady, who gave birth to me, and my late grandfather who was praying for me to be a girl. This brings my story to my birth in Kokomo, Indiana, and of my God's sovereign opportunity for me.

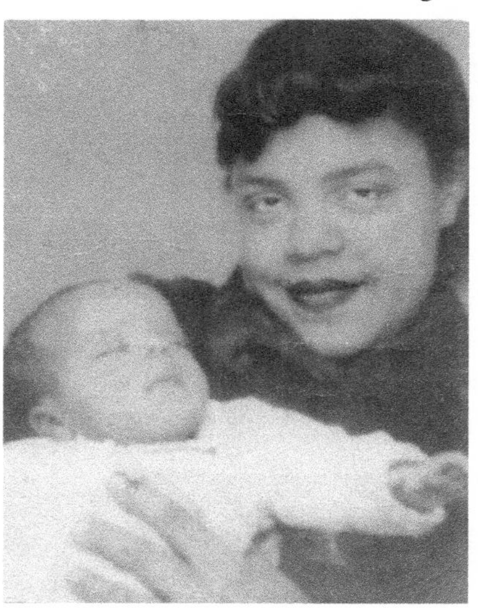

My late mother Margaret E. Smith Grady, & baby Robert Cornelius Grady

I entered this world on January 17, 1939, as Esther Emogene Grady. I am told that I was placed in the outstretched hands of my mother, Margaret Smith Grady, and my father, George Grady. Then I was put in Grandpa Duke's hands as he performed the historical tradition and actually held me up like Kunta Kinte as seen in the movie *Roots*. He blessed and committed my life, my predestined (such times), into the loving hands of our God. It was the first anointed stage of opportunity waiting for me.

What did Grandpa Duke do next? He took off running, barefoot, through the deep Indiana snow (without me, of course) on a street that I like to call the Hallelujah Avenue (Cooper Street Hill), hollering, "We got a great long gal!" When I grew up, I was always the tallest in my class.

Before I go any further, I am encouraged to share the representation with the people in my life and the similarities of the characters in the book of Esther.

The following are the character representations (reflections):

- *Mordecai*—my Uncle Bill, most wonderful encourager in my time of need.
- *King Ahasuerus*—the authority figure that releases favor given by King Jesus. Divine favor was given to me when my praying grandmothers first introduced me to Jesus. They willingly dragged me to church when I was unwilling to go.
- *Haman*—life's carnal fleshy thorn. The "Haman" in my life represents all the deceitful manipulation and hindrance known to man that were against me.
- *Esther*—the called, chosen for God's "such times". Colossians 2:9 says, "For in Him dwells all the fullness of the Godhead body." Esther's heart searched for the fullness and righteousness of God to do the right thing for her people. She desired God's given purpose to be complete as she walked into her destiny.

Preparation is "an act of processing unto readiness for a specific purpose(s) to be made suitable" and being "equipped with the necessary provisions according to plan."

Stage is "a period, level(s), degree(s) in a process of development, growth, of change; made suitable for presentation(s)."

As I share many areas in my life, I thank the Lord that I am free to do so. Hopefully, the freedom I now experience will open the floodgates of heaven for other people to receive the freedom that they desire. The biblical Esther had provisions in her preparation stages. I also had my provisions and total belief that God would open the doors for future manifestations.

A. Esther's time of preparation was twelve months, which was suitable for King Ahasuerus and also for Haman to uncover his plot (Esther 2:12).
B. Although my preparation time is for a lifetime, it was very evident that preparations were taking place within the first twelve years of my life before my mother passed away. I knew that Jesus would never leave me nor forsake me. In all the initial stages of life, it was first covered by my mother's love like no other. My praying grandmothers were very significant in my life as well. For the scripture says the prayers of all the saints continue to go up (Revelation 8:3–5).
C. I was thirteen years old when my mother passed on June 20, 1952. Uncle Bill, a deacon, played a very significant role in my spiritual life especially. He watched over me every day during my preparation stages as Mordecai diligently watched over Esther during her time of preparation.

This is a special dedication to my mother, Margaret Smith-Grady, from this chapter's point.

In the little time I had living with my parents, I watched over my mother during her time of illness. She had been nearly blinded from rheumatic fever and put in a dark room at the age of thirteen, but she overcame her diagnosis. She wore thick glasses, and she suffered a heart condition all her life. We truly had a treasure in her earthen vessel (body).[6]

Mother cried often but did not pity herself. She was one hard worker with Daddy. She had the hearts of many people from all walks of life. I now understand that my *anointed times* of preparation began with my mother. Because of the time and area we lived in, my

---

[6] 2 Corinthians 4:7.

mother was the first black body that was received by a white mortician named Peacock. He preserved her soft, pretty pink skin against such a pretty pink dress that the city had never seen. You know how a child never forgets such things.

I had such love and compassion for my mother, especially for her determination and dedication as a hardworking business woman. She was a notary public and had great public relations in owning and operating their local restaurants and grocery stores. It was in the 1940s and grocery stores—some awesome kind of PR was working for her! And in those days, her notary public was like a lawyer position in the '40s and '50s! We did find all kinds of law books when she passed! She was her church's pianist for a while—at Wayman AME Zion, Kokomo, Indiana. It's a shining example of preparation stages for me, how God wants to continue using us to *his* glory!"

For most of my childhood, I was living with my grandparents, shifting back and forth, and also with my Uncle Bill, who was my teenage help until I left home! With vivid memory, I even remember when my parents would send me off to stay with these very nice lady friends from church. They all looked after me as if always praying for me! "Hello! *Now*, I truly know to say, 'Thank You, Lord!' The song says, "Somebody prayed for me, had me on their minds! Yeah, Mamma and Grandmamma Nem!"

My mother was the oldest of five living siblings.

Now the late Mary Jo Smith, the late James L. Tompkins, Mildred L. Lewis, and Bertha M. Paul—all of them had college education except her. My Uncle James Onion (smile) was one of the first black men to attend the US Army Academy at West Point! They all loved mother dearly, and she loved them! "You all children are watching!" I saw them feeling so helpless, wanting to do more than they could for her in her infirmities. She knew they were touched (Hebrews 4:15); however, she was a tough cookie! By the way, she had named my daddy Cookie (smile). Mother had that bold personal directive from the Holy Ghost bought with a price—a sold-out life to Jesus Christ! (1 Corinthians 6:20).

George Grady 53 yrs. old
My Daddy after he had
forgiven my trick on him!

I saw my daddy following through with just about anything they were to do in his own man's way of hard work, especially at the steel mill! One day, I saw him not being supportive enough, and as he lay sleeping in his recliner after work, I let a fly land in his open mouth! As I kept looking at this pretty gold-capped tooth! I guess I lost sight of it flying, whether accidentally or on purpose (smile)! Well, I wasn't an angel!

I always felt so sorry when I did anything wrong! Just know, it was godly sorrow unto repentance (2 Corinthians 7:9, 10). I do know that I did not do it again and truly learned from it! Even now, the confession and reminder of it is good for the soul! Nevertheless, I do not like to do harm to anyone nor see wrong done to them! And when even back then, they did wrong to me, I forgave them over and over again (Matthew 18:21, 22). It's even more relevant since then in my spiritual growth and dying-daily Christian life! I pray to always remember that God's Word says "To whom much is given, much is required" (Luke 12:48) and also that by growing faith in His living Word (Romans 10:17). He has promised me of His anointed provisions throughout every challenge of my scepter-touching life!

All I have to continue doing as more and more is given to me and as the enemy is allowed upon me more and more (Romans 7:21) is to believe and trust in Christ Jesus as if my life depends upon it, knowing that "He shall never leave nor forsake me" (Hebrews 13:5B) and never forgetting to say about the hindrances of others, "Father forgive them, for they know *not* what they do" (Luke 23:34, emphasis mine).

All these very things have been so impressionable upon me through my mother that the more I'm sharing them with you, the more revealing and freer I am becoming! Hallelujah! It's as if I am also led to receive the same spiritual baton through the presence of the Lord of my mother's same Holy Ghost of God's anointed scepter touching for my life! Yes, how these things slowed her down! The beautiful pink flower she represented was allowed to be nipped prematurely in her fragile life.

My mother's preparation stages from the 1940s to the 1950s (my "such times") and Grandma Joy, a local dear friend, may have been God's will or His Divine favor for me to be able to write this book. I also know that writing this book has unlocked many areas of my life that I would have taken to my grave as well. If there is anyone who desires to tell a story of their life's journeys, please seize the moment and don't neglect the gift that has been given to you. Please check out my friend Grandma Joy Whitaker's most wonderful book(s). She is a most inspiring encourager and children's storyteller and destiny image author.

The deeper I get into this section, which is about my mother being the preparation stage for me, I have to admit that I have always felt the need to be in prayer with the Lord. With my mother dying at the young age of thirty-three, the thought of death lingered in my mind until I reached the age of thirty-three. A few years ago, my sister, my brother, and my children shared the same comments about themselves. In January 2006, I praised God when I turned sixty-seven, which surpasses the age of thirty-three twice. I definitely do not take these privileges for granted.

During the challenging times of my life, my spiritual growth has increased each day in my personal preparation stages with God. The Lord encouraged me to stand on his "yea and amen promises" in my preaching and teachings, living more and more of a blessed life through my praises to Him. "Let all the people praise thee" (Psalm 67). I believe in good health for God's people among all nations and for souls to prosper (3 John 2). I recall a message from Jackie McCullough as she preached of Psalm 67 in 1995 at the Woman Thou Art Loose conference. As we nestled down for the message, we were told to "stand on God's promises like a hen over her biddies to be hatched." We must trust in God with great expectation and always give praises to our Lord, knowing in whom we have committed our lives and circumstances to and fearing nothing. Psalms 68:1 says, "Let God arise and let His enemies be scattered." Our responsibility is to love and pray, even for them.

We end this chapter with some of my mother's comments that she shared with me during my early preparation stages that I will never forget. Maybe you can relate to some of these humorous yet practical tips:

1. Do not leave home without making your bed. You never know who may have to bring you home.
2. Always wear clean socks or hosiery.
3. Never leave home without wearing clean underwear.

4. "Jeanie [my nickname], keep your dress down and your pants up!" My mother got a kick out of this one, but just repeating it can be a tongue twister! Smile!
5. Give your soul to God before it's too late, and encourage mankind everywhere!

Chapter Three

Chosen Feelings

"Am I doing what I am supposed to be doing?" I wonder if Esther asked this question to the Lord. I believe that she did, and the Lord said to her, "I will never leave you nor forsake you" (Hebrews 13:5).

1. Have you ever had the feeling where you said to yourself, "I believe I've been here before"? Does it feel like your destiny is out there somewhere and is waiting to meet you face-to-face?
2. Have you ever felt like your life's purpose is tugging at you to meet your fulfillment?
3. In Romans 8:28, we know that "all things work together for good to those who love God, to those who are the called according to His purpose." Verse 29 tells us that we are predestined. Are we predestined because we are chosen? *Chosen* means "picked out by preference, selected, theologically elected, favored by God." We know who we are, and we also know through the scriptures that we have been called and chosen by God.

God, who knows our end before our beginning, may have looked at Esther's choices like this: Esther chose to believe that God was going to provide for her through her tremendous measure of faith. She also knew she would be accountable for the request that she made on behalf of her people. Esther must have realized the favor that was upon her because of her obedience. Remember in Luke 1:28 when Mary was chosen? Her spirit agreed, and she knew that she was chosen and highly favored by God.

We Were Predestined (Chosen)
Similarly Viewed Relations

Hallelujah!
Isaiah 40:31; Isaiah 62:10; Jeremiah 1:5

Esther (Her Family's Side)

Esther's Grandmother
Esther Lorraine Tompkins
March 1, 1900 (birthday)
Esther's Mother
Margaret Elizabeth Smith Grady
January 20, 1919 (birthday)

Her Mother's Oldest Sister's Name
Mary Jo Tompkins Smith
October 1, 1921 (birthday)

Nine (9) years between Esther
and her brother Robert "Bobby"

Robert (His Family's Side)

Robert's Mother
Lucille Wright Perara
December 1, 1900 (birthday)
Robert's Oldest Sister
Altae Mae Cliette
October 16, 1919 (birthday)

His Youngest Sister
Mary Sue Graham
July 29, 1921 (birthday)

Nine (9) years between Robert
and sister Mary Sue

Esther was born January 17, 1939 Robert was born November 22, 1932

Our birthdates are always on the *same* day of the week but *seven* years apart. *Esther* married *Robert* Perara. Her grandmother *Esther* married her grandfather *Robert* Tompkins.

The other *Roberts* in Esther's family are the following:

- Their youngest son, Robert "Bobby" H. Perara Jr.
- Her nephew Robert "Rob" C. Grady II
- Altogether eight in total with the above
- Her brother Robert "Bobby" C. Grady Sr.
- Her late grandfather Robert "Daddy Bob" L. Tompkins
- Her late husband, Robert "Bob" H. Perara Sr.
- Her Aunt Bertha Paul's son Robert Paul
- Plus, her brother's wife Shirley's late brother Robert Lamar
- Shirley's son-in-law Robert Russell

The *Esthers* in Esther's family are the following:

- Herself—Esther E. Grady-Perara
- Her late grandmother Esther "Mama Essie" Tompkins
- Her late auntie Baby Esther Tompkins
- Her Aunt Mildred's daughter Esther Angela Tompkins-Lewis
- Their daughter Margaret Esther Perara

The *Margarets* in Esther's family are the following:

- Her late mother, Margaret Elizabeth Smith-Grady
- Her late great aunt Pastor Margaret Robertson
- Her sister Norma Elaine's daughter Margaret Goudy-Smith
- Their daughter Margaret E. Perara
- Robert's godmother (the late) Margaret Young

The *Lucilles* in both families are the following:

- Her late great aunt Lucille Fort-Bell
- Her late stepmother Lucille Jackson-Grady
- Their daughter M. Lucille Perara
- Her husband, Robert's, mother, the late Lucille Wright-Perara

The *Marys* in both families are the following:

- Her late auntie Mary Jo Tompkins-Smith
- Their daughter Mary L. Perara
- Her late sister-in-law Mary Sue Perara
- Her husband, Robert's, grandmother Mary Stokes-Wright

The Henrys in both families are the following:

- Esther's late husband, Robert Henry Perara Sr.
- Their son Robert Henry Perara Jr.
- Esther's late uncle William Henry Grady
- Esther's late uncle Henry Fort (also the grandfather of Paul Warfield, 1979 retiree of the Cleveland Brown Football League, and sisters)

Esther's cousin Mordecai was a true encourager. It is such an honor to know that the Holy Spirit encourages us daily. The Bible says, "For in Him, we live, move, and have our being" (Acts 17:28). Mordecai's heart to encourage Esther gave him the credibility of hearing from God and being obedient. God purposed for Mordecai to have a profound and predestined movement of faith with the result of also providing him with a "chosen feeling."

1. We still believe God's Word even without seeing the word *God* written anywhere in the book of Esther.
2. We believe in this awesome, most exhilarating, dramatic, and history-making Bible lesson of all time. Even today,

it continues to bring forth thoughts and dreams of the decision Esther had to make.

3. We need to truly believe that Mordecai heard from God and gave Esther the encouragement she needed to save God's beloved people so the Jews (the lineage of Jesus Christ to come) would not be extinct. Whether Mordecai heard from God through the cloud by day or the pillar of fire by night or God's audible voice, he obediently heard Him.

I come to a screeching halt at this point to pray for our men of God. Men, with all this talk about Esther, please know that you have been chosen. You have the privilege to hear God's voice clearly. Are you hearing the Lord's voice today? This chapter could have been dedicated to my Mordecai, Uncle Bill, or to my late, loving, and dedicated husband, Robert.

Meanwhile, Mordecai's representation of God is to encourage a chosen generation (1 Peter 2:9), even for today. We need more of our men of God to take a stand and handle family affairs in our lives again. The next generation needs to hear your voice. The anointing of the Lord must have been flowing in Mordecai's veins as Haman tried to kill God's anointed people (1 Chronicles 16:22). We see the favor on Mordecai as well as on Esther. For all his courage against the Haman spirit, we see him covering for Esther as he voluntarily fulfills his responsibilities to her. Mordecai was devoted, honorable, courageous, and loyal to his calling. The similar attributes and leadership style is needed in every Christian home (even dysfunctional) today. By the way, this book's last chapter (10) was first thought to be "Please do not forget Mordecai"!

Men of God, as you hear the Lord speaking to you, please know that the women of God stand ready to support you and truly have your back. More importantly, God has your back also. Remember, our theme scripture for this chapter says, "He will never leave nor forsake you." Men, women of God are also cheering for you more than you know. It is our heart's desire to know that we are one in Christ and we are on one accord with the kings and priests of our homes. Matthew 18:19 says, "Again I say to you that if two of you agree on earth concerning anything that they ask, it will be done for them by my Father in Heaven. "For where two or more are gathered together in My Name, I am there in the midst of them." Men and women should pray that we recognize the mighty force that we are when together in Christ.

When Mordecai was in trouble and grieving because Haman was pressing upon him, we immediately saw teamwork in action. The sackcloth-and-ashes[7] response he displayed was too much for Esther to bear. We see her going to God in prayer.[8] Then they gathered all the Jewish people together, ensuring they were on one accord, and fasted and prayed for three days.

We need to pray for those in authority as instructed in 1 Timothy 2:1–2 so that we may all live a purposed life. The war-ridden days from July 2006 and beyond certainly needed prayer. Our men, regardless of the race, shall not be extinct. Are we praying enough? You are chosen by God, and the scepter is extended for such a time as this. It is time for us to do as Romans 4:17 instructs us to and start calling those things that do not exist and speak it in existence.

I do know that some men give up more easily, feeling so beaten down. There is often little encouragement and more criticism spoken against men. This proves useless in the fight against a Haman spirit, which is the enemy within. He may feel so beaten down that he may not even want to get back up. Then there are times when the man is running away from his spouse's nonsupporting tongue.[9] I'm sure there have been many encounters that have taken place in this area of a relationship between two people. As the man slowly dies spiritually, he may even eventually leave home or commit wrongful acts. We must understand that we cannot force a man to talk and they are not going to be forced to talk. Based on my experience with Bob, men also need a lot of proven encouragement. Sisters, together we can help put those negative feelings in men to rest.

It is important that we are standing on God's holy Word and all the promises contained therein. I was determined to share my uncon-

---

[7] Esther 4:1–2.

[8] Esther 4:14, 16.

[9] James 3:8.

ditional love of God with my king and priest (Robert) in his days of chosen moments with us. God's divine favor certainly began falling on me. Robert's hidden chosen feeling (as macho men sometimes try to fight against) was brought to spiritual fruition before leaving here on December 11, 2002. I stood on 1 Corinthians 7:14, believing that the unbelieving husband is sanctified by the believing wife. Robert and I celebrated our lives together. Haman's evil spirit was dead in our lives (Esther 9:22). At our huge fortieth wedding anniversary celebration on August 25, 2001, we were very happy to share our "anointed such times" with our children, our friends, and our family members. It was a chosen moment at its best. To God be the glory!

Robert told people he was married the right way this time (our second time of celebration), and then he was saved the next day. For any doubting women, please look at what God did in my life. A husband that previously warned me not to go into ministry decided to become my greatest supporter, which launched me into my most humble chosen moments ever. I preached my initial sermon the next day on Sunday, August 26, 2001. By God's grace, my Robert was able to witness it. The Haman spirit in his life was dead. He was 100 percent changed. My sermon title was "What Price the Anointing," and my subtopic was "It Costs Something." Robert attentively watched and listened as he heard every living Word of God in me. I am sold out to Christ forevermore. This glorious day of redemption was a chosen day of deliverance for me and for Robert. Hallelujah!

Our wedding theme was "the marriage supper of the Lamb" (Revelations 19:9). The design of our wedding invitation cover confirmed everything for us, which was "The Table Hath Spread: Robert and Esther's Fortieth Year-Feast of the Lord Is Going On and On and On" For we are not ashamed of the gospel of Jesus Christ, for it is the power of God unto salvation.[10] The night of my initial sermon was a new beginning. God's living Word certainly freed me and also Robert unto his departure on December 11, 2002. The chosen feeling we shared prevails forevermore (Matthew 16:18–19). To God be all the glory!

---

[10] Romans 1:16.

Chapter Four

Going for Broke: Ministry Is No Joke! You Are either Ready or Not!

Esther's very house of birth Kokomo in 1939

Jeremiah 1:5 says, "Before I formed you in the womb, I knew you." This verse speaks to my spirit about my ministry before the foundation of the world.

My destiny came right down my street, up my walkway, and knocked on my door at 205 South Cooper Street in Kokomo, Indiana. My destiny jumped right from my mother's womb, into my parent's hands, and to my grandfather's hands, waiting to bless me. As previously mentioned in chapter 2, my Uncle Bill helped to raise me later in life. All the men in my life have been blessed by the Lord eternally and have "gone for broke" in ministry in such vulnerable times of my life.

Going for broke means to go all out for the Lord, to not settle for things in life but embrace the Lord's purpose and destiny which He called us to. Additionally, God's master plan has been very conducive to my life. He knows my end before my beginning. It was His opportunity to combine my preparation stages with my chosen feelings and my "going for broke" mentality for such a time as this.

It wasn't until recently in my adult life that I understood just how purposed I really am. Previously, I was unable to see myself as God saw me and catered to a sense of low self-esteem. But God's plan for my life prevailed. It is not about me; it's about Christ.

My grandmothers, Big Mama and Mama Essie (my mother's mother), took care of me for a while after my mother passed away. My oldest brother, George Everett Grady (nicknamed Porjie), was always in reform schools, jails, and prison. Porjie would always comment that he was down on his luck, but I would rebuke it by saying, "God loves you and wants to bless you—it's not about luck." He was so mixed up in life that he thought some of the things he was doing was actually pleasing to God, but it was very clear that it wasn't. When it all came out in the open, the things he had failed just broke his heart. Porjie had gone in a different direction in life, which was not God's way.

The only thing I could do for him was to pray that he would turn his life around for Christ's sake before it was too late. I always hounded him to seek his salvation, not knowing then that a person cannot be pressured into making a life-changing decision unless they are ready. Thank God for His mercy. He allowed Porjie (George Everette Grady) to leave this world, giving his life to Christ. Thank you, God, for answering my prayers. Even though he was in pretty bad shape—both legs amputated, riddled with diseases, and on dialysis—God still redeemed his soul, and he was received in the loving arms of Jesus. I believe that George E. Grady's redeemed soul was a manifestation of God's grace. We're just continuing in the blessed Calvary . . .

I used to encourage Porjie to receive Christ through my brotherly love for him. My brother could have been turned off by my persistence and rejected me and my message about Christ, his soul possibly lost. Porjie was something else, but God is God. I went for broke because of the Lord, and Porjie was able to receive Christ. I knew the Lord had His hands on this, but I quickly learned that I will never attempt to push Christ on anyone else ever again!

God was allowing things in my life to move at a fast pace. His scepter touched my life, and His anointing made it easier for me to love people unconditionally. I am sold out to Jesus Christ, and going for broke allowed people to see Christ in me and not me. We do not know what (or who) is standing spiritually before us. Hebrews 13:2 reminds us that the stranger before us may even be an angel.

It was extremely hard on me not having my mother around even before she passed away. My parents went away at times on jobs together. I was so blessed with having caring and loving grandmothers. My grandmother Mama Essie fulfilled the role of a mother. I was privileged to be around her beautiful daughters (my aunties) who were my age. Even though I was surrounded by love, I was still a vulnerable child.

I had a tremendous complex that wrestled with my emotions and caused me to feel like no one really cared about me. Perhaps it had a lot to do with being engulfed with fire by my brother when I was four years old. Please refer to Chapter Seven! I later came to realize that Jesus Christ is with me (never leaving nor forsaking me) and that I could overcome it all. As I matured in my spiritual life, I learned how to deal with my emotions and the pain. I embraced Philippians 3:13–14 and pressed toward the mark for the prize of the high calling of God in Christ Jesus.

When I was at Mama Essie's house, I came to realize later just how much appreciation I owed her for the challenge of putting up with me. She was truly a sold-out, anointed, and loving woman of God who was definitely committed to caring for her family.

I also came to realize that although I was timid and never intended to give anyone trouble, Mama Essie disciplined me right along with my aunties. Mama Essie kept her long braided cowhide rope hanging up in clear view on the doorway of the dining room and would not hesitate to use it if necessary. The girls would always have me hollering about something, and Mama Essie would come after all of us, swiping at us as we flew under the huge dining room table to keep from getting hit. The funny thing is that all of us kept a secret—we would make sure the cowhide rope would hit the table legs to avoid hitting us! Oh, how funny is that? Smile!

My insecurities grew at night because my aunties would tease me and wait until it was dark to say, "I see two big eyes." I would start to scream, and Mama Essie would come up the stairs. There weren't any night lights in my earlier days, so we had to tolerate the darkness. I'm sharing this with you in hopes of helping the timid, nonvocal children out there.

I was a little bit younger, but the Lord kept saying, "Keep loving them. You know they love you. Children will be children." I couldn't stay upset long and found myself saying about anybody about anything, "Father, forgive them, for they know not what they do." They really didn't know what they were doing, but I knew they were good girls at heart and that they loved me.

Mama Essie, late Esther Tompkins and her sister that raised her
Late pastor Margaret Robertson

I resolved later in life that it could have been worse for me, but God was always with me. My quietness could have easily made others think I was withdrawn, but there was no running to the psychologist back then. My grandmother and her sister, Reverend Margaret Robertson, started the Pentecostal Holiness Church and dragged us to church seven times a week, including three times on Sundays! Yes, Tavis Smiley knows about these days in Kokomo, Indiana; they were sold out for Jesus and were spiritually bold. They really went for broke.

In the summer of 1952, I saw my mother fading away in the hospital. Everyone around her would always say, "She cannot hear you." I guess without disrespect to the elderly, I would always tell myself, "The hearing is the last to go." For Grandma Nem could not make me believe in a million years that my mother was not responding to me. I told her that I know what she was saying to me, "Jeanie, take good care of my babies." She was referring to me over and over in my mind. I know very well that my siblings Bobby and Laney are in charge of their own lives and souls, and they are still going for broke this very day. My siblings are in their fifties, but they are still my babies. If you are a mother type, I know you understand.

Esther's sister Norma Elaine Goudy and the late brother Robert C. Grady Sr., and with me

My brother Bobby remembers our mother's last words to him as she was seizing the moment. Although she was very weak as she was being taken to the hospital, she still said, "Bobby, be a good boy." Well, he is still good and truly a man of God today. As parents, we must be careful what we share with our children. Bobby had just turned four years old in April 1952, and our mother's words to him were very memorable ones. He would always see that moment as a moment of "anointed such times" in his life. Since then, my beautiful brother Robert C. Grady Sr. passed on to glory in 2014.

In school, I was always picked on by the boys for being so quiet, and they would always call me googly bear. Jesus was always there to console me; therefore, when I looked in the mirror, I didn't see what the boys saw. I had to encourage myself in the Lord at a very young age. My mother passed, and it was hard enough being a motherless child during this time. Everyone is eligible to give encouraging words to a child (even when parents are unable to). Remember the golden rule: "Do unto others as you'd have others do unto you." On July 21, 2006, I was blessed to be able to attend my fiftieth class reunion at Kokomo High School in Kokomo, Indiana. Even though I was picked on by some of my classmates when I was younger, I was very excited to see everyone at the reunion. I had great expectations and love in my heart for everyone who attended the reunion. It was truly a milestone and a moment of "such times."

I also went for broke during my days of marriage. I was married twice in my life and persevered in the first one until the weight of our marriage nearly broke me. I hightailed it out of New York and didn't look back—not once. I was determined not to be among the eight million and one story in the Naked City! I was very saddened by the experience, but it helped prepare me for the anointed times I was about to encounter.

When my first husband and I divorced, we had two lovely children to come out of our blessed union at the time. Keith (the oldest child) was three, and Kevin was two. It is always wise for us (the parents) to consider how the children are watching us. We need to instill in them that the Lord shall lead, guide, and direct them in their journeys. We must teach them to not do everything we do but to practice what the Word says to do for the sake of their own soul. Although 2 Corinthians 6:14 instructs us to be equally yoked, it has always been difficult for many of us to find the right relationships or loved one even today.

One thing about children is that they truly are a part of the consequences of divorce without being able to avoid the stress of the misery, heartache, and confusion of an unsuccessful marriage. We need to help our children understand why their parents are getting a divorce. It is a start to share with them that it's not their fault, but they must believe it. All of us make mistakes, and we are not perfect. All of us should charge ourselves to be set free from our sins. My pastor, Bishop Smith, would always say, "If you mess up in your life, remember Romans 3:23. We all have sinned and fallen short of the glory of God." We need to confess our sins, truly repent in godly sorrow, and get back up again. We need to clean up, give ourselves to Jesus by surrendering everything, and then go forth in Jesus's name (Romans 10:9, 10). Why do millions of people make repentance so difficult in life?

When I accepted salvation in Christ, I was truly able to follow our Lord's model prayer (Matthew 6:12), for the Holy Spirit helped me forgive my ex-husband. I had to forgive him because I needed the Father to forgive my debts (Matthew 6:14) and I needed my children to believe in the Lord and in me. I truly needed the Lord to help me forgive him of his trespasses—the same as I want my Heavenly Father to forgive me for my trespasses (Luke 6:28). We must bless those who curse us and pray for those that spitefully use us (Luke 6:28). Blessed are the merciful, for they shall obtain mercy (Matthew 5:7).

Well, although I did not have contact with my ex-husband (the father of my two oldest children), I have never failed to pray for him whenever I prayed for my second husband. It was important to pray for his salvation. As I stand before my Lord and Savior, I do not want to recall having a tormenting day in my dealing since, for I have the peace that only Christ Jesus can give. I am so free (John 8:32, 36). I went for broke during those "such times."

I further share with you the old saying "I'd rather fight than switch." Well, I had to prove it by not switching away from my Jesus and all he has been to me. I made a decision to have a true relationship in Christ and not revisit the world's idealistic values. Going for broke, I was so serious about the Lord that I was compelled to portray Christ, even before Robert. I'd rather go for broke, not bowing to sell my soul to the enemy in this subtly deceiving and sinful world anymore. I didn't even want to play an innocent game of bingo, which I played in the past for almost thirty years. It was a love for the habit I had even before meeting my second husband, Bob (Robert), and it was a habit he really enjoyed tremendously, then us together. Stay tuned!

I would take a chance on playing bingo for fleshly gain instead of trusting God and His faithful ways, which sometimes keep us from surrendering to His will. We should totally surrender to God and not choose to love and do what we desire, for our God is a jealous god! I too wasted time going after the things the world had to offer and was jeopardizing my soul (Matthew 16:26) in the process. I know it was the Lord's will that I decided to go for broke. As for me, I chose not to continue my bingo habit, which put me in hot water with Bob, but I had to keep my faith in knowing that I was doing the right thing!

Women of God, while waiting in sheer determination for God, I walked around Bob with a silent, nondeadly tongue. I marveled at my pastor, who reminded me of my favorite saying, "A blessing delayed is not a blessing denied." Two weeks after Bishop Corletta Vaughn's powerful revival in December 1992, I gave up bingo. Bob suffered a pulmonary edema, went into cardiac arrest, flat-lined, and miraculously came back to life on January 3, 1993. Well, I knew God was not through with him yet. Seven years later, on May 30, 2000, I received the rewarded blessing God promised me as Bob finally received his salvation in Christ! Bob's salvation was definitely something to shout about. Hallelujah! You couldn't give me a million dollars to play just one more bingo game. I loved it more than anyone I knew, but I resolved not to play with God, and I knew God sure was not playing with me. I am not saying that making a decision to lay down the game of bingo was the reason Bob gave his life to the Lord. I do believe, however, in obedience and order in all the things that God requires of me. All of us should charge ourselves. "Look at what the Lord has done, I am now more determined than ever to go forth in Jesus' name!" Going for broke!

Meanwhile, back at the Holy Ghost ranch, I knew my life was fit for some serious kingdom building as I went for broke and sold out to Christ Jesus for ministry. God had me right where He wanted me, which was to be solely dependent on Him, and I loved it. Most of my family left the Indiana area. I also left Indiana and moved to North Carolina, a place where I had no family. I had to totally depend on God. It wasn't easy, but I know it was the plan God had for me (Jeremiah 29:11). The Lord knows my end before my beginning. God also knew that all the things that I had to walk through were in preparation for my ministry.

While I was in the care of my loving family members (during my mother's illness), I was initially baptized at the age of five in a hometown church in Kokomo, Indiana. I was baptized at five different churches, but I know they meant well! I do recall the one experience that will stick with me forever. The church of my grandmother Mama Essie's church was a Pentecostal Holiness church. After a baptism, we would spend hours on end (in those days) for the power of the Holy Ghost's anointing. I didn't quite understand what was going on and would peep at everybody, even my two aunties. I saw a lot of people falling out. Little did I know until it was revealed to me in my adult life that tarrying for the Holy Ghost was unnecessary the way we used to do it in the past. God will not hold it against them all! I learned since an adult, how my daily power needed comes from having chosen to receive the Holy Ghost's spirit of Christ- which is Jesus! (Romans 10:9–13).

Jesus is still true to His Word, and He honors our faithfulness very seriously. I had something within me that I could not explain, and it was Jesus. I was five years old and trying to make sense of all the things that had taken place in my life. The Lord kept showing me that He still loves me and I am to still love Him and others unconditionally for the rest of my life.

I had received the Holy Spirit with His anointing and power flowing through me. It is the "such times" of my life that I knew I was being used to God's glory. He has revealed to me that I am not to discount those precious days of old. He shared with me that Mama

Essie's and Big Mama's spiritual eyes were steadfast upon me. God is too wise to make a mistake, for He knows everything. My end before my beginning was in the making, and I'm signed, sealed, and delivered for the Lord's sake. It was as if I was visualizing Esther going in to the king, knowing that her life was going to change dramatically. I submitted my life to King Jesus when I too had gone up and proclaimed Him as my own, along with my aunties. It was truly an anointed time in my life.

As my second husband, Bob, and I move forward, I have one huge positive outlook and attitude during our military life. Bob and I were raised up the same way. My commitment was easier for me because I willingly yielded to Christ's anointing. I knew that I was to trust God in loving my husband, Bob, and I knew Bob's heart. His favorite song for a long time was "It is no secret what God can do; what He has done for others He'll do for you."

Bob always got a kick out of sharing the story with other people of how we first met. We were out dancing at the local facility. and as Bob would say, "I was fitting in the groove!" Later that evening, the musician was playing my favorite instrument, the saxophone. The musician, an acquaintance of mine, asked me to dance during one of his breaks, with Bob just knowing I'd say yes. I answered, "No, thank you, I promised him [Bob] the next dance." Yes, I had game for them at least. Smile! And I know that God has long forgiven me for the little lie I told. I was playing hard to get for as long as I could. The joke was actually on me, for I fell hard for Bob soon afterward! You see, he still found me (Proverbs 18:22). He/we always laughed about the story and that night. Well, sisters, even though I might've strangely tended to his ego a bit that night, watch this: just as sure as King James Version's Proverb 18:22 reads, "He who findeth a wife findeth a good thing and obtaineth favor of the Lord," the *eth* means to continue on being. We are to just continue being that good thing that they found. The ball certainly was in my court. For my faithful "going for broke" life was very well determined (as he found out) to honor that favor unto my husband! Loving and obeying our God in each our own different circumstances! Guess what? In all of this setup for our marriage, Bob played the thing, just knowing I would be honoring the good, loving examples of the women of God in my life's training—mainly my grandmothers. He loved them dearly, and they certainly thought the world of him. He was such a good old-fashioned husband and father type.

Robert and Esther courting stage on the Beach!

The Lord, through this book, is revealing the meaning of Hebrews 13:5b: "He shall never leave us nor forsake us." No matter what He allows us to go through! "Remember His own Son on the cross of Calvary?" All truly was not lost, for Jesus arose, giving us all a chance for eternal life!

Well, to this modern-day Esther, as He desires to be to all of us Esther spirits (man, woman, boy, and girl), He's available for every bit of touching the spiritual scepter of God needed in our lives! Only He knows how our lives are predestined to turn out. It's just up to each of us how they are to end up with whatever Esther spirit of encouragement needed in our "anointed such time" lives! Remember now that the anointing is the very presence of God through Jesus Christ—the anointed one with the anointing power for our needs.

Getting back to how Bob and I began, Bob had already tried to get me to notice him when I was out selling Avon products, but

I politely shrugged him off as just another Air Force fly boy, as the older local people would call them. They thought these fly boys would come in town and try to influence their young daughters, granddaughters, nieces, etc. Some of them married and departed the area which for the most part ended up as a favor, for many of them would not have had a chance to even go to college. I entered into my destiny, believing that "all things work together for good, to those who love God, to those who are called according to His Purpose" (Romans 8:28). I knew I had been predestined to be with Bob (Romans 8:29). Refer to chapter 3 "Chosen Feelings."

The military was very good to our family in many ways. We learned patience, responsibility, endurance, tolerance, and certainly togetherness. We grew very accustomed to different nationalities, activities, and events that the base communities have to offer. The unity in the military extends from the soldier to the family members in learning how to become one. Our family had an appreciation that Uncle Sam does not tolerate prejudice or discrimination.

Military personnel are committed to working side by side each day to successfully accomplish the mission or task that is issued to them. Respectfully, we need the same type of unity in our daily lives and in our churches. It will continue to be very difficult for the body of Christ to become one glorious church without His unity (Ephesians 5:27). I am grateful that the military world and the civilian communities are coming together as one. I have witnessed both organizations praying together and supporting the needs of each other, especially the needs of our soldiers, who are at war and fighting for all our freedom, and their families. Thank you, Mr. President Barack Obama, Michelle, and the Bidens! Also others whenever in office.

I now understand how my early childhood days were just a setup in teaching me how to persevere in life. Allow me to share a little about my recent years of how my ministry materialized. My husband, Bob, whom I had to surrender to God in every aspect so that I could grow in my Christian walk, had no idea just how much I too needed my future career nurtured. I was motivated by the unconditional favor of God, for this man knew how to provide for his family and was also very career-minded. The military and his mother made sure he was taught how to care for his family. He never asked for much for himself at all. Although many of our circumstances are different, please know that with the help of the Lord, all things are possible.

My journey was not easy, but I willingly made sacrifices and waited on the fulfillment of God's promises. Although I had great love for the Lord, I was denied the freedom to speak the name of Jesus in our home. I was also denied reading the Word in the house. Nevertheless, Bob still supported me, taking the children to Sunday school and to church. At times, he would even attend church with us. I just did not nag him!

My patient late Rev. Hubert R. Hunting,
& his beautiful supportive family

I also thank the Lord God for allowing me to care for the elderly for thirty years as a caretaker. In my twenty-third year, I knew God was calling me into ministry. In the last seven years as a caretaker, I worked for one of the most inspiring and understanding men of God, Reverend Hubert Hunting (also known as Rev). Rev had fifty years of pastoral ministry as a Southern Baptist pastor. He was paralyzed and needed a lot of special care (no eating, no walking, and very little talking). Realizing he no longer needed his initial ministry materials, he blessed me and gave them to me. I was so grateful to receive the material; however, he did not stop there. He also paid my way through ministry school for most of the first two years. I truly thank God greatly for Rev's generosity. Stay tuned!

Since the beginning of that particular season of my life, Bob saw more and more manifestations of Jesus Christ. On my graduation day from ministry school, he saw God's amazing grace at its best. I graduated with honors, with all As. He told me, "I never knew you had it in you." The Lord let me come back with "You never gave me a chance to show you." In the beginning, Bob was unable to understand my need for ministry. Two years afterward, he supported me, and only then was I able to flourish in the life of ministry.

I am very honored and blessed that Bob was an amazing husband, father, and provider. He used to tell his troops on their Airmen's Proficiency Report, "If you put out, I'll put on." In other words, if you do a job well, he will always take care of you. I believe this is what God is telling us. We should "walk by faith and not by sight" (2 Corinthians 5:7), remembering that we do all that we do because we love Him—going for broke.

Eventually, my blessing that was delayed but not denied manifested. Like I said, at least one year before his passing, Bob supported me in every aspect of the ministry. He said, "If I can't beat them, I might as well join them." I knew God was having some serious conversations with my husband. He had changed 100 percent and even said to me, "Jeanie, when you get your church, I'll be your assistant pastor." Hallelujah! This moment was part of his sold-out, life-changing decision to be a partaker of the gospel. In fact, Bob and Reverend Hunting became great buddies until Bob passed on December 11, 2002. Bob had to learn to go for broke, like Reverend Hunting did years ago, touching the scepter of God for His anointing!

I knew I was witnessing to Christ's newly transformed servant, my husband, Bob (Romans 12:1–2). "Oh, it is Jesus." It confirmed all I would have to know about the Lord's validity of my sold-out, "going for broke" ministry, which God has for me. As I previously stated, ministry is no joke. You are either ready or not.

Chapter Five

Watch Out, Haman's Gallows, My Eyes Are on Jesus

When I think of my family's commitment to military life, I am encouraged to remember that "if it had not been for the Lord on my side, where would I be?"[11]

There is an old familiar military saying that "Uncle Sam ain't no woman but sure can take your man." It is not a cliché but a lasting truth. As long as there is a military, there will be wars. The Bible says, "And you will hear of wars and rumor of wars" (Matthew 24:6). I feel that this scripture gears our military into a sense of readiness and preparation for the potential possibilities of future wars against our nation. I thank God that our armed forces are always mission-ready.

My Robert
Late Chief Master Sergeant
Robert H. Perara Sr.

My husband, Bob, was sold out in the military with an attitude that required his troops to make it happen. He loved the military, and more importantly, he loved his troops. He was a chief master sergeant (CMSgt) superintendent of several squadrons during his career. Bob's leadership style was no-non-

[11] Psalms 124:1–2.

sense (hard but fair), and the soldiers that worked for him respected his position. His motto was "Let's get the job done and do it right the first time."

You didn't have to be a genius to work for him, but he was a stickler for people having common sense. He was not too impressed with soldiers or senior leadership who carried a lot of book sense only, as he would call it. In fact, if he had to choose between a soldier having common sense versus one having book sense, he would select the one with common sense hands down! Bob would say, "I can't use someone in the air force who knows it all and doesn't want to learn anything. That's the individual that would get my whole squadron killed. He might as well go across the line and fight with the enemy." I would crack up every time I think about his comments and the way he would say them.

There were times that his military outfit would have to go temporary duty (TDY). Their TDY assignments would usually require his squadron to be deployed for six months to a year, and their departure could occur at any time.

Everyone respected Bob and called him by his rank—chief. A chief master sergeant is the highest enlisted rank in the air force. Bob certainly was a no-nonsense man. He was known to never argue a point that he couldn't back up in black and white (on paper) and that you couldn't take it to the bank. Also, he stood faithfully in teaching our children military responsibility. Our children can relate to the type of leadership style Bob stood for. He was very hands-on and would not think twice in getting his hands dirty to show them how to do something.

Bob had a heart to teach his troops and his children how to be the best they could be in anything they attempted to achieve. His heart to teach reminded me of Jesus teaching the disciples to wash one another's feet. The Bible says, "If I, your Lord and Master, have washed your feet, you also ought to wash one another's feet. For I have given you an example that you should do as I have done to you" (John 13:14–15). With my husband's wisdom, knowledge, hardcore military mannerism, and deep, roaring voice, he had a serious demeanor of taking names and calling roll!

God, through His Holy Spirit, led, guided, directed, and comforted me. Bob may have had a bark, and I knew not to try his bite; you see, I knew his heart, and I truly loved and respected him. He took his role as a responsible husband and father very seriously and certainly his military career! Yes, to each his own, but I learned to yield when I needed to yield and found the balance in our marriage and in our family. Sometimes the ability to yield was necessary, and there were times it required me to grin and bear it. All these events were predestined by God, which also increased my faith in Him—definitely Esther's anointed "such times"!

The Bible says, "He who is in you is greater than he who is in the world" (1 John 4:4). The Haman spirit will always try to come between a husband and wife, for they are the foundation in a healthy family. True relationships must prepare for spiritual warfare. The enemy does not want a family to succeed. It is a spiritual battle, but the battle is the Lord's (1 Samuel 17:47). We must keep our eyes fixed on Jesus, for our promise is perfect peace (Isaiah 26:3).

My husband resembled the stature of General Russell Honore, who gallantly led the troops through the Hurricane Katrina disaster relief efforts. Bob and General Honore have an amazing resemblance in stature. Whenever I saw General Honore's wife on the television, I just prayed. I may not know her personally, but I can identify with the pillar of strength she has to be for her military husband. It takes a very strong woman to understand military life. Bob would always comment that I was his E-10 (a promotion he made up, considering that the rank of E-9 is the highest rank for an enlisted member of the armed forces) as well as being named the air force chief status, another air force name for E-9. He made me feel like we were truly a team. But believe me; it took a lot of touching the spiritual scepter of God!

Bob also felt that *many* of the youth in society could have benefitted from a four-year enlistment into the military. Over the past twenty years, it seems as though children have lost respect for adults and walk around with an attitude. He felt that military manners would be good for most of today's youth. I always agreed with Bob on this approach. Four out of our five children joined the military (two in the army and two in the air force). The military was truly a way of life for our children. I am definitely not stating that they were perfect, but I can safely say that our children experienced a very cultured way of living along with learning how to have respect for others.

Cliché in the beginning of this chapter means "stale, tired, worn out, without freshness, etc." The Haman spirit is always working overtime against our military families and *any* family unit! Many years ago, a military man or woman was called a GI (Government Issue) and was instructed to protect the government. Sometimes, military men and women can feel that the accomplishment of the mission is more important than a soldier and their family. Although a soldier is very clear on what type of occupation they signed up for, it doesn't make it any easier to go to war and leave their family behind. When the soldiers were discharged from the military, some of them were financially broke, disappointed, and ready to throw in the towel. It is very critical that the spouses support their love ones with the spirit of Esther, who shared her compassion and love for her people. Haman's spiritual gallows have no place in the anointed times of this modern-day spiritual Esther, who is touching the spiritual scepter of God. My eyes have been on Jesus!

Bob retired in 1978 with twenty-seven years of service. He passed on December 11, 2002, after living twenty-four years in between. After his retirement, he was employed as a truck driver for Maola Milk Company and also worked thirteen years as a Wayne County school bus driver. The average post-life expectancy for military retirees in the 1970s and 1980s was five to ten years. Our family prayed that he would be blessed with a longer time frame. However, it was very difficult for a military retiree or discharged soldier to find employment once they departed from the military. Job loss in a military family (as in all families) created more stress in the home. I pray that our military families continue to place their trust in the Lord. God is the only one we can count on during the transitional season in our lives.

Isaiah 10:27 prophecy says, "And all yokes shall be destroyed because of the Anointing oil." We should speak the Word every day, proving ourselves to God that we believe in His provisions and in the

Holy Spirit. Proverbs 18:21 says, "Death and life are in the power of the tongue, and those who love it will eat its fruit." Esther spoke life into her circumstance. My family learned to speak life over our situations even when trials and tribulations occurred. God is divine and always faithful. Whatever seems too hard for us, it is just right for God. I decided to be a living sacrifice. Romans 12:1 says, "I beseech you therefore, brethren, by the mercies of God, that you present your bodies a living sacrifice, holy, acceptable to God, which is your reasonable service." Let's speak God's promised words into the atmosphere.

The spirit of Haman did not want to see the Jews live. It was a spirit that entertained dying and death. Men (both military and civilian) are private and may not share their innermost feelings. Changes in life that they experience may make it difficult for them to feel comfortable to open up to their spouses or family members. We have to pray that the Haman spirit (lack of communication) is broken from our men. The freedom to communicate must be taught to the men of the next generation and thereafter. Wake up, women, with these young sons!

The military is well known for unity, security, and service to our country. The military man also has a responsibility to protect his family as well as his country. It is God's desire for all men to be the king and priest of their home. The spouses also have a responsibility that is very significant to the kingdom of God. We must pray for peace for our spouses and keep our eyes fixed on Jesus. When we strive to promote peace in our homes, love and communication are surely to follow not only for the military families but also for everyone.

The love of God, truth, prayer, and communication are critical elements necessary to keep any family together. Let's focus on the military family for a moment. There are many military families that are unable to cope with life in the armed forces. The pressure is on when the service member is called to take an assignment that is away from their family for a period of time—sometimes several months to a year or longer.

The Haman spirit would love to see marriages fail, careers destroyed, and children devastated. The enemy is after relationships, period. For most military soldiers, there's pressure to meet specific time lines to be promoted to each grade in the military. A promotion comes with increased finances. These finances are significantly lower than a standard job in private industry. The family (which usually consists of three to five children) is forced to stretch their limited finances until the next pay period. As with any family, most of the arguments that are generated between spouses have to do with lack of finances. The pressure is on regarding stress. Adding to the stress is the dynamics of the job itself. Some of the details may include maintenance of a fighter jet, juggling the dangers of loading or unloading bombs or strategizing war plans. These dynamics or combinations could send anyone over the edge. It takes a teaming effort consisting of prayer and faith to prevent the enemy from winning the battle between a married couple and their family. Is there anything too hard for God? No! So go on and touch His spiritual scepter by faith and belief! And we say, "Watch out, Haman's spiritual gallows, our eyes are fixed on Jesus!"

As we see in today's church age, there is a significant need for many prayers to be answered. We are to remember to pray with clean hands and a pure heart.[12] The Bible says, "Let brotherly love continue."[13] In the Bible, 1 Timothy 2:2 also says, "We all may lead a quiet and peaceable life in all Godliness and honest reverence."

Jesus talked about everything; actually He has such a heart for us to love one another. There is a new move of God in today's churches and in our homes. I am hopeful that many of you will join me in covering our military men and women (all over the world) in constant prayer. Our military soldiers are gallant, brave, dependable, and committed souls that sacrifice themselves to protect their families and the United States of America. Let's make a commitment to fast and pray for their strength, protection, and increased relationship with the Lord and then with others!

The military has its shares of peaks and valleys. There were several times that the military was very challenging for my family, espe-

---

12 Psalms 24:4.

13 Hebrews 13:5.

cially with its famous motto: "Uncle Sam ain't no woman, but he sure can take your man!" How did we make it? Prayer and love was the true source of our strength, and it allowed us to make it through the tough times by all of the promises of the living Word of God. I know in my heart there are military spouses that can relate to such necessities. We are all in this together, and the military needs our support in all of our "Esther spirit's anointed such times"!

I have learned how we must let the enemy know who we are in Christ every time he tries to come up against us. Philippians 2:9 says, "God has highly exalted Jesus Christ and given Him the name which is above every name." There isn't any reason why we should let anyone or anything take us under and try to kill our spirit. In my imperfect life, I have experienced doubt, fears, and unbelief; but I made a commitment to repent, continuing to die daily of the carnal flesh (1 Corinthians 15:31) and rid myself of any spirit that may try to distract me. Christ has already given us the victory over our foes with His promised love for us. Therefore, I continue to learn as the Lord allows me to be tried and tested. The harder the devil is after me, the stronger I become in my Lord Jesus Christ. I have to remember 2 Timothy 2:12, which says, "If we endure, we shall also reign with Him; but if we deny Him, He also will deny us."

The Esther spirit experience is to strengthen and encourage God's people. Esther's heart represented the living church within the church communities with her bravery and courage through all the snares encountered! Through the Haman spiritual gallows in our many devastating days in the military as (more than ever before) many lives are maimed and lost, we all can at least pray as we feel the cost together! (Iraq or anywhere)!

Yes, as we see in today's church age, with the many prayers needing to be answered, it is best to make sure that we will all, through this Holy Ghost power, pray right! Keeping our spiritual eyes on Jesus will surely get our prayers through! Remember (Psalms 24:4, 5; 2 Timothy 2:22) to pray with clean hands and a pure heart, especially those walking in (Hebrews 13:1: "Let brotherly love continue") into the anointing presence of Christ Jesus (Hebrews 13:5)! Yes, remember Romans 15:1, "Strong bearing the infirmities of the weak," especially in covering those others and praying for all of these needy men/women! So like 1 Timothy 2:2 says, we all may lead a quiet and peaceable life in all godliness and honesty! This is definitely for His (Romans 8:14) Spirit-led women for these men! All will benefit! Jesus has said (about everything actually), "I will set the rest in order when I come" (1 Corinthians 11:34B).

(Men and women, even those leaders not leading with a new church age spiritual, walk with a newness of life!) When not in this walk, Romans 8:1 says we're not in Christ Jesus and are setting up our own condemnation! We're just charged to pray for them all.

I am sure many of you do touch and agree with me on God's will. His way for especially today's prayer covers His faithful, giving, devoted military men and women stretched all over this war-torn world! With their gallant, brave, dependable, committed souls, they sacrifice for families and all of the United States of America and then also for allies, wherever needed in our Father's world!

Everyone, I stand ready to testify of the goodness of the Lord in helping to maybe free others in part. I know my family and I certainly did need all we could get against every ole Haman's evil protégé and the spiritual gallows threat in every one of Esther's manifesting "scepter touching anointed such times" through fasting and much prayer!

Prepared for all of the enemy's full steam sheath tricks:

1. When a mistake is made, especially on an aircraft, it costs millions! It even affects the leader in charge, sometimes mightily!
2. Military men/women are devastated when their stripe(s), which is a component of their makeup are taken! According to an old military saying, "it always takes longer to sew a stripe on than it takes to rip it off!"
3. It's the same type of devastating torment with finance and accounting messing with their money!
4. And then those sudden oversea assignments come up (hot spot or not), some covered up.

   a. Often these are isolated tours, where family cannot go!
   b. It leads up to one highly important issue, some spouses saying, "I have my babies to care for and the house is falling apart every time you leave." It's *chaos*!
5. The spouse says, "I'm going home to Mama!" And sometimes they stay there, losing the right focus over the Haman spiritual gallows!

The only reason I am releasing these helpful nuggets to you is that, in being helpful, I am hopeful that the wars identifying with you out there, especially military spouses, will be over! For your families sakes, and those deep war wounds within, many are praying for your belief that there is Hope! Believe no negativity, just focus on Jesus, claiming, declaring, and decreeing in anointed victory that help is on the way! Esther truly sinched it for me, with her courageous oneness mentality in her needy time of revealed corporate sold-out fasting and praying! Sooo significant for me, this God allowed (through the grace of Jesus Christ) New Testament/Church Age privileged cause of Christ for within us being able to portray His loving desire (especially the anointed prayerful women of God), that, "We all may be one!" (John 17:21)

Also, all of this releasing was done so that you—the loving, concerned, caring sister or brother citizens—could know just what some things are that we military-affiliated people need prayers for in support whenever these come into our minds. If nothing else, say, "Lord, your will be done!" Yes, we're in it all together as God's children, giving to Jesus, the Son of the Living God, to be all as one in His Spirit! To keep our eyes focused on Jesus together, we need you out there!

In addition, I have learned how we must let the devil know who we are in Christ in order to keep his goose cooked every time he is allowed upon us and ours! And in speaking Philippians 2:9 (God gave the highly exalted name of Jesus Christ over every name in Haman's spiritual gallows), I learned that everything's got a name! Hallelujah! There's no sense in me letting whomever/whatever take me under—like when visualizing a drowning man with his helpless but hopeful hand raised up in the air! Well, the song that comes to my mind is how Jesus (whom we are to keep our eyes focused on) shall spiritually and physically in His will rescue the dying and save the perishing! Right, Esther? It's in your scepter touching "such time" (Esther 4:14, 16).

Oh no, this Esther is not perfect; she has doubts and fears no less than any of you! She is just repentant in dying daily (1 Corinthians 15:31) and in ridding the ole spiritual gallows of carnal flesh, a hindrance in all our trust in the Lord! He has already gotten us the victory over every conquered foe with His (Romans 8:37) promised love for us! Amen. I continue to learn how the Lord allows the tests in trying me; well, the harder the devil is after me, the stronger I become! Hallelujah! I then have to remember, in whatever pain, how 2 Timothy 2:12 says, "If we suffer, we shall also reign with Jesus, but if we deny Him, He shall also deny us."

Even in all this likely unsettling in your minds, we Esther spirits are to experience our Lord God's strengthening and encouragement of His "scepter touching anointing such times" for each of us, the family of God, because of Jesus!

The Lord hath revealed unto me how Esther of Shushan's days represented the living/working church within the churches, it is most highly likely that we are to take advantage of this Old Testament guideline of Esther's courage in going forth to God's glory by saving His Beloved Jewish people—yes, in the saving of God's family, which is the very lineage of the earthly Jesus, who is to come! It befits us all. "Ole Haman's spiritual evil protégé gallows" can be defeated over and over and over again! Hallelujah!

Anything of God, letting go and *letting* His Holy Spirit (like in Acts 17:28, Him living, moving, and having our very being) just trips "ole Haman's evil protégé spiritual gallows," although he returns again and again (Matthew 4). He just cannot stand it, especially when these lovely military families take beautiful advantage of "Esther's scepter touching anointed such times" of gaining such good rapport with people from all walks of life, races, and nationalities. Amen. Our entire family benefited from such, having been raised up to have no differences!

The Lord hath just been with us, "never leaving nor forsaking us" on every hand! (Hebrews 13:5 B). We're to continue by faith, believing in the goodness of Father God and *just reflecting where* we might be *if it had not been* for the Lord on our side! (Psalms 124:1). We just thank God Almighty as we *go for broke, "selling-out to" Jesus* one after another!

I suggest you try Him today, (Colossians 2:9) the fullness of God *in Christ Jesus*! Inasmuch as **I** keep *my* eyes on Jesus, *I* rely *on Him* to anoint *me* for such times *in my life* for my family's sake! God bless you and yours!

Chapter Six

God Meant It for Good

Haman's evil spirit was no match for the Spirit of God upon Esther and in me now!

The word *evil* spelled backwards is *live*. The enemy desires for our thoughts and decisions to be backward, heartless, and without purpose. God desires that our destiny is full of life, love, and passion for Him and His people. In Genesis 3, the deceiving serpent beguiles Eve as she was being tested. His tactics obviously were quite deceitful, and he meant for his actions to be *evil.* Every situation we go through, God meant it for our good and to test us. God desires for us to *live* through Him, relying on His Word and to be in communication with Him.

Deuteronomy 8:2 says, "And you shall remember that the Lord your God led you all the way these 40 years in the wilderness to humble you and test you, to know what was in your heart, whether you would keep His commandments or not." God was testing the Israelites to see if they would keep His word in their hearts. The magnitude of their tests was enormous. The enemy meant all their trials that they went through for bad, but God meant it for their own good.

If we rise up together in unity and the fullness of Christ is in us, we will be able to overcome our tribulations. When a person has committed a sin, it is our responsibility to pray for them. We should pray, "Father, forgive them, for they know not what they do." We know that the plans of the enemy is to challenge the love we have for God every day, for it is Satan's strongest desire to see all of us fail. Are we ready to take the spiritual charge for godly living that the Lord purposed for us? Everyone who desires to live right opens their minds to become more Christ-like. Redemption (Genesis 3:15) and salvation allowed us to be brought back and saved so we can be one with the Father through Christ Jesus. We thank God that He turned evil around and permitted us to live! We thank God for Jesus!

The evil forces upon the children of Israel consisted of constant mumbling, grumbling, and complaining, which eventually wore Moses down. The disobedience of Moses was triggered by the constant attitudes and actions of the Israelites. Moses became angry and made an error by striking a rock instead of speaking to it. This decision prevented him from entering into the Promised Land. In spite of his actions, God still blessed him eternally. The proof of Moses receiving eternal blessings is written in the Bible during the transfiguration of Jesus Christ (Matthew 17:1–5). Even though striking the rock prevented Moses from walking into the Promised Land, Moses was still blessed. God meant the things Moses walked through for His good.

Haman tried to utilize his evil thoughts against Mordecai and Esther. Haman's actions backfired on him. He was put to death instead, and the Jewish people were not destroyed. The Jews, the very lineage of Christ, were spared from God, who truly turned it around for His good and allowed them to *live*. God will always have our backs if we remain obedient to Him.

Another excellent example regarding evil mind-sets at work is the story of Joseph's brothers in the Bible. In the book of Genesis, Joseph was loved by his father, Jacob (Israel), very much but was hated by his brothers. They wanted to kill him, but they threw him in a pit instead and told their father he was dead. Joseph was later pulled out of the pit by his brothers and (Genesis 37:27) sold into slavery to Potiphar. He was later favored by God to interpret the Pharaoh's dreams, which allowed Joseph to become the prime minister of Egypt, second-in-command only to the pharaoh (Genesis 41:40). Joseph is a perfect example; the enemy tried to take him out, but God meant for Joseph's journey to be for good! Joseph humbly forgave all his brothers, who wanted him dead. Joseph was not only favored, but his entire family (including the brothers that hated him) were also favored. Joseph's story is truly phenomenal! His story is bigger than him and not just for him. Hallelujah!

In the book of 1 Samuel, God allowed one wife of Elkanah (Peninnah) to torment the other wife (Hannah) because her womb was shut and she was unable to conceive. Hannah kept praying with a humble heart and worshipped before the Lord. The Lord opened her womb, and she vowed to give Him her unborn child, Samuel, to the Lord for all the days of his life. When Samuel was born, Hannah kept her promised vow to the Lord and gave Samuel to Him (1 Samuel 1:19–2:1). Samuel was born to live a life serving God and His people for all of his days. Peninnah meant it for evil, but God certainly meant Hannah's testimony for His good!

God does not want us to incur our debts. Currently, this is another example of the enemy's desire for our lives. Even though it is a sin for families to overspend and take on excessive amounts of debt, God can still use this for good. Our errors as adults can always help us to teach the next generation of debt-free living. God never meant for His people to live poorly or be irresponsible with our finances.

Professor Damieon Royall taught us to "stay in the living Word of God, seek His Face, and you'll get what He's got in His Hand." We want what God has in His hand for our lives. We must forgive ourselves for the debt we incurred that we weren't supposed to take on. If we repent, truly ask the Lord for forgiveness, and move forward to debt-free living, God can definitely use all our challenges for His glory. Lord, it is my prayer that we live in the life you have purposed for us. Bury our temptation to spend and live outside of our means so that we will not always be a borrower but an eternal giver. Amen.

Everything we walk through is meant to be for the Lord's good from the beginning of time. There are times when we get in His way and we can't blame everything on the devil because sometimes we give him access. Our decisions to let the enemy have access are not intentional; however, it still happens. John 10:10 says, "The thief does not come except to steal, and to kill, and to destroy. I have come that they may have life and that they may have it more abundantly." The first part of the scripture speaks of evil; however, the second part speaks of life!

Did God allow evil to happen to anyone more than His only begotten loving Son, Jesus, at Calvary? Even at His crucifixion, Jesus was concerned about His adversaries and asked the Lord to forgive them.[14] He sacrificed it all for us to be loved from our sins. God's heart is for His people to be faithfully and spiritually connected with Christ Jesus in heavenly places with Him (Ephesians 2:4–6). Romans 8:28 says, "All things work together for good to those who love God, to those who are called according to His purpose."

I believe in God's promises and how important it is to submit to Him and resist the devil (James 4:7). We know that the enemy will flee if we resist him. When I was younger, the enemy tried to create havoc in several areas of my life, but God meant it for His good for me. Allow me to share with you a rebellious decision I made that hurt my loving Christian grandmother, Mama Essie (the late Mother Esther Tompkins). Initially, I did not have an appreciation for my God-given name, Esther. My grandmother's name was Esther, and I didn't care to have this name when I was younger. I didn't understand the significance of the name or what it really meant to her. I always recalled how most people identified Esther with Sanford and son's Aunt Esther.

Mama Essie's lifestyle was filled with true worship for the Lord and carried many similarities to Esther in the Bible. I made a decision to be called by my middle name, Emogene, or as Bob would call me, Jeanie. A few years ago, I attended my fifty-year class reunion. All I kept hearing was Emogene. After all these years that have passed, it had finally affected me that I should have loved the name that I was given, which is Esther.

There is truly something about a name that is given to us. I pray that parents are very selective in the names they give their children. I didn't understand the significance of my name, Esther, and therefore missed the meaning of the name. I don't believe that Mama Essie held it against me. I truly repented, and I had to forgive myself. I love the biblical Esther, and I have gladly embraced my name. For the past thirty years (while living in North Carolina), I have been called by my name Esther and have been very blessed that it is the name that God wanted me to have for all of His "Anointed such times" for me!

---

[14] Luke 23:34.

As I previously mentioned in chapter 4, my late brother George Everette Grady (Porjie) felt I was always hounding him about being saved. My witness to him was very different than my witness to anyone else. I had to put up with a lot of his wrongdoing also, but I was determined to make a true difference in his life. I was sold out for Christ, which ironically began with my relationship with Porjie. It brought me closer and closer to God and to Porjie also. I was so glad that he received Christ into his life! My sister, Laney, helped coach him. I witnessed it on the telephone when we were stationed in Guam while he was in the Veterans Hospital in Indianapolis, Indiana, and Porjie even won another soul to the kingdom before he passed. God is good all the time! The devil tried to permanently trap my brother's mind, but God meant it for His good. The Lord let him live eternally with Him. I thank God for all that He did for Porjie against all the evil.

My first husband (the father of my two oldest sons, Keith and Kevin) took me to live with him in New York. We tried to make the marriage work, but it was unsuccessful. I learned from my mistakes and was determined to move forward. I was married to my second husband, Robert (Bob), for forty-one years. He was the father of my three youngest children: Mary, Robert Jr., and Margaret. Although some of our years were difficult, many of them were wonderful. Bob truly was the love of my life. He provided love, support, and discipline to all our children whether they were biologically his or not.

We had a wonderful marriage; however, Bob was on a journey to find a relationship with the Lord for many years. Spouses that know the Lord know that it is a hard thing when one spouse is faithfully waiting for the other one to reach their salvation in Christ. I stood on the Word, knowing that God is forever faithful and just. He knew everything that our family needed. He knew that Bob needed to be the king and priest of our home. As I waited patiently for Bob to find Christ, I continued to let the Lord strengthen my own walk with God. I learned, learned, and learned! I stayed in the Word and pursued Christ, which led to my life in the ministry. There were times where agreement between Bob and I was not initially exercised in this area, but nevertheless, I knew I had to press forward anyway.

My forty years of prayers to the Lord were finally answered, and Bob received his salvation blessing before parting this earth. The last few years of his life were paramount in Bob's salvation, and so were his support for me in the ministry and for having the love of Christ in his heart like never before. God truly used me for His glory, which forever blessed my husband and our home. I praise the Lord for turning Bob's life around so he can live forevermore. God meant for these cherished moments to be for His good in our walk with Him, the true meaning of "to God be all the glory" (John 12:23–28). For just as God got His glory from Jesus being on the cross in Calvary, He gets His glory from our sacrificial, faithful lives too!

My daughter Margaret Esther Perara Avey w/ me at my 50th Class Reunion Kokomo In 2006

Please allow me to revisit some details regarding my fiftieth class reunion in Kokomo, Indiana. My daughter Margaret made our reservations for the reunion three months in advance. We get together as much as possible (my brother Bobby gets a kick out of our resemblance and my daughter Mary also). Little did I know at the time that I needed Margaret's support more than ever before!

Two weeks before attending the reunion, I acquired a gout meniscus knee that I simply could not explain. The pain and pressure was so excruciating; it was hard to press down as I walked. I told my children, "I might have gout knee, but it doesn't have me." I prayed and prayed (as I was still determined to go) and said, "Lord, Your will be done." Although I was in pain, I was still able to attend the reunion, but it was by touching the spiritual scepter of God for this anointed such time. The Northwest Airline and US Airways wheelchair service was also a blessing to me. They ensured that I was off my feet as much as possible.

I met up with Margaret, who flew in from Virginia. We bonded at my fiftieth class reunion more than anywhere else before. I truly wanted for nothing while I was there, and my classmates enjoyed her as much as they did me. Just as my brother Bobby gets a kick out of the resemblance between Margaret and me, my classmates were overwhelmed by it. Our family time in Kokomo was also special. I count it all joy (James 1:2) in the Holy Spirit, for God meant it all for His good for me and still does. Dear hearts, please remember the Old Testament's Esther. She believed in saving her Jewish people. I pray that we are believing God for our family's salvation, maybe redemptive manifestation and for mankind everywhere. I also pray that we are believing for great commission empowerment and a mighty move of God. We must also believe for the salvation for people. Jesus is the only way, the truth, and the life (John 14:6). My prayer is for their spiritual walk.

I am even more aware that the destiny and purpose for our lives will be brought to fruition. I realize more and more that our purpose is about Him, and I am completely satisfied with the direction and path He has chosen for me. Families and churches and my pastor constantly remind us of stewardship to our Lord. We must have faith to believe in the passion of God for the church family. If we truly believe that God meant it for good for all of us, then we must believe for being in Jesus Christ.

Chapter Seven

You Reap What You Sow

I spoke of my dear sweet mother in chapter 2 and my gallant and faithful Uncle Bill in chapter 8. I would be remise if I did not speak of my loving grandmothers, who loved me and kept me in church by the will of God.

Special dedication to my grandmothers, Emma Grady and Esther Tompkins. They lived out God's living Word that was purposed for their lives. The promises of God radiated in the hearts of both women, and I am eternally grateful I had them in my life.

My spiritual, praying grandmothers charged right into their missions. These women were complete, perfect, and made whole in their relationship with the Lord, and they wanted the same for me. My grandmothers remembered all the things that Christ had done for them. They were tremendous witnesses for Christ. When I was a little girl, I was dragged to church even when my fleshly mind did not want to go. My grandmothers were fruit-producing women, and they were determined that this mission (me) would be a successful one.

As I glimpse back over my life, I know my grandmothers were instrumental in my walk with the Lord. God's grace and their faith became a true team. When it came time to pray for me, they prayed. When they needed me to learn the Word, they taught it to me as much as they knew how. When my grandmothers needed to show me how to apply the Word to my everyday life, they rolled up their sleeves and showed me, and oh, how they lived it! Revelation 12:11 says, "And they overcame him (Satan) by the blood of the Lamb and the word of their testimony, and they did not love their lives to the death." My grandmothers overcame many things during their era, and I am grateful that they shared their testimonies with me.

As a young girl, my grandmother's testimonies taught me to always walk in Jesus, for one day I will have a true testimony to share with my generation and my family. My grandmothers leaned on the everlasting arms of God and trusted in His holy Word. God never failed them, for they went very far in life by their faith in the Lord. They understood Romans 10:17: "So then faith comes by hearing, and hearing by the Word of God [which was living in them]." Lean on means incline in motion-of-heart, of mind, and will (like) toward depending on Jesus Christ, pressing forward relying upon him. My grandmothers pressed "toward the Mark for the Prize of the High Calling of God in Christ."[15] It's my church's theme right to this day!

Emma Grady (known as Big Mama) was a very humble and beautiful woman. She was also a loving and giving person that I truly respected. She faced many things in life, including past challenges, but with God's grace, she was able to overcome them. I loved my Big Mama and respected her submission to the power of God. She knew who she was in Christ, and she surrendered every area of her life to the Lord daily. She was truly a legacy.

My great grandmother late Harriet Hateher Fort 1800's

Big Mama sought the Lord's help in overcoming something that her mother (my great-grandmother, Harriet Hatcher Fort) told

[15] Philippians 3:14.

her. During the time of slavery, my great-grandmother told Big Mama that her husband had to witness a painful assault. She told Big Mama that he had to stand by while a taskmaster gave a thumbs-up approval for one of his men to rape her (my great-grandmother). Big Mama found out that her mother was still able to keep her after she was born. Even though it was a tragic incident that was very hard for Big Mama to take in, she was importantly a forgiving woman. Big Mama also learned to forgive through life's challenges. She would talk to other women (even me sometimes) in teaching/sharing how to be free from all kinds of pain caused to us. What a spiritual-Esther anointed-of-God provisional witness, especially to me, Big Mama and Mama Essie were later on. God only knows their many necessary lifetime needs of touching the spiritual scepter.

However, Big Mama's marriage to my grandfather was truly a test. I loved Grandpa Duke, and I was his little girl. In chapter 2, I expressed the bond that we truly had since I was born. There were many challenging times that took place between Big Mama and Grandpa Duke. I won't go into the specifics, but I wanted to express the respect and love I have for my grandmother. I watched her stand in her marriage even though there were times her heart was broken. She taught me how to put my total trust in God in every area of my life, especially when I get married one day. Her strength in the Lord taught me how to also have strength in Him.

Big Mama was resting her innermost part in God. He promises us that He would never leave us nor forsake us regardless of our circumstances. I recall another incident in her life. One day on the farm, she helplessly saw my daddy fall into a field thrashing machine. God spared his life. He had many surgeries, along with a lasting limp and hump in his back.

When our first daughter, Mary, was born, Bob and I had to decide to move from Big Mama's house, where we stayed. We needed to look for a larger home. Like in chapter 2, she would have been able to relive the joy of Grandpa Duke's Kunta Kinte's experience with me. She cherished the thought of having that moment with her first great-granddaughter. After we left the hospital, we stayed in a larger house with our two other children. Mama Essie would always say,

"Give Daddy what he wants," and I know Bob heard it too. Smile. Every time we took Mary to visit Big Mama's house, she filled Big Mama's heart with joy. In sharing her life's challenges, I wanted to also share her ending.

Esther's grandmother Emma Rene Fort-Grady, 2 days before passing-on!

On Big Mama's last day with us, my cousin Billy said she raised up and pointed to the window. He asked, "What are you pointing at, the cemetery?" She said, "Uh-huh." And she went home to be with the Lord. It truly hurt his heart when she passed, but he knew she had to go. I was miles away, living in Guam, but I also knew it was time for her to be with Christ. Thank God that all her sons were saved and went home to kingdom's glory also. Even though she is gone, I know her spirit is still praying for me. Prayers of *all* the saints continue to go up (Revelation 8:3–5). I truly love Big Mama, and I know that she loved me.

My other grandmother, Mama Essie, was one in a million. She was more outgoing and similar to Esther in the Bible. Mama Essie truly loved the Lord, glorified God, and was a very loving and caring woman.

She honored her family as a she nurtured her loving and devoted father of 110 years at her house during his later years until he passed. His name was Reverend Everette "Pappy" Rhorer, and he was a pastor. She also cared for her older brother, Uncle Roy Rhorer, a World War II veteran and hotel chef. She cared for her younger brother, Uncle Ray Rhorer, a Korean War veteran and railroad conductor, and her sister, Reverend Margaret Robertson, also a pastor. Lastly, she truly provided tender, loving care for her loving husband, Robert "Daddy Bob" until his passing. God was really good to Mama Essie for all of her family was saved. I certainly thank God for her "anointed such times" in her much-needed "touching of the spiritual scepter of God"—life!

As a little girl, my unconditional love for God kept my mind intact during some very difficult times in my life. The tests that I went through set my praying grandmothers on a spiritual course like none other that I've seen since. The dysfunction that my brother had against me nearly tore my sickly mother's heart apart. We were about to embark on a lifetime of sowing and reaping, though I did not believe for mine to be for the bad! Although I spoke of my stepbrother's passing (Porjie) in previous chapters, it is important that I share a specific experience in this chapter with you.

One of Mama Essie's greatest tests was to see her grandson (Porjie) choose salvation in his life. My stepbrother was very much at odds with me. I was unaware of him being a stepbrother and was unaware of the jealousy he felt for me until I was an adult. The details that I am about to share regarding my brother Porjie have been included in my book with the sole intention of helping someone that has been devastated by an incident in their life. I truly pray that the experience I am choosing to share may help a person that is identifiably struggling with unforgiveness toward another person or family member.

When I was only four years old and Porjie was five and a half, his father owned a grocery store. He did not want me to go with him to get candy. On one particular day, I remember Porjie took a flaming cardboard box from the trash pile (in the back alley) and commenced to slinging it on me. My mother immediately ran to me to throw a huge white sheet from the clothesline over me (which seemed like cotton). After the ordeal, I had burns over 75 percent of my body. It was because of no one but God that I only ended up with a little scar on my forehead, one on the right side of my face near my ear.

Unbelievable as it sounds, Porjie tried it again! This time, Big Mama ran into the kitchen as flames were shooting up my yellow dress. I couldn't even believe what was happening to me! It was so horrific, and I felt like I didn't know this person at all. From Esther's "anointed such times," I remember the flames but not the pain. Hallelujah!

I need to describe Porjie's character to you. Porjie received many beatings for his constant wrongdoings. The more beatings he received, the worse he would get. He was always sent home from elementary school. One of the things he used to do in school at a very young age was dip a girl's braids down in the inkwells on the desk behind them. The Georgie Porgie nursery rhyme gave him an edge with little girls. "Georgie Porgie, pudding and pie, kissed the girls and made them cry." Porjie did everything you can imagine. He began reform school at eight years old, and my mother would take me with her to the jail and prison to see him. The passion I have for the prison and street ministries today is because of the experience that I had with Porjie.

Every beating Porjie received caused me to feel sorry for him (but still love him) more and more; I was unaware of his continued jealously for me. Every time we would walk down the street, the neighborhood dogs would growl, which would scare me tremendously. When I screamed with fear, Porjie would beat me. I would even try to pull his buttons off to make him stop, but that didn't work. People would see us and say, "Here come Porjie and Jeanie." I later found out that my sickly mother could hardly take it anymore, and that was the reason why she would send us over to her mother's house or her friend's houses. My grandmothers tried tirelessly, in their way, to talk to him, but it proved unsuccessful each time. They did not call on a psychologist in those days. Mama Essie's husband, Daddy Bob, would take him to the coal shed, calling it the library. Lord have mercy, the outcries were horrible as Porjie was always hollering for Mama. Sometimes, I can still hear it to this very day.

One day my father was fed up with Porjie. He put a dress on him and whisked him down the street with a broom! I certainly do not condone this type of discipline on any child, but my father was at his wits' end regarding Porjie. My grandmother's hearts broke, but they kept praying for Porjie to turn his life around. My mother would just cry nonstop, and her heart condition continued to worsen. As Porjie worsened, God continued to show me something that was vitally important. Through all of the drama Porjie displayed, he knew that he had the unconditional love of my mother and grandmothers and me as well. Porjie knew they would always pray for him. They were sowing the seed of prayer because it was the one thing they would always do for him. They were sowing the seed of prayer because it was the one thing they knew would bring a positive result. My grandmothers knew that the results may not happen overnight, but their time of harvest was only going to happen through prayer in God's own way/will/time!

I was always around my brother somewhere—yes, in Esther's "anointed such times," truly touching the scepter of God! The Lord later revealed that sometimes I was being used as a support system for Porjie. One evening, while I was in my teens, we were at a restaurant. The police were called on Porjie for no reason. Although Porjie was not guilty this time, he was still taken away. There is always two sides to a story; however, when you have a police record, your word is not believed nor trusted. Porjie had lots of rebellion and had resisted arrest in the past. Porjie was furious and was not cooperating. From the results of that day, wasn't our Lord's "anointed such time" certainly with him then and in my humble covering? Hallelujah!

As the police dragged him to the car, he got away and went home. I followed close behind him all the way. When he arrived home and did not receive any support from Daddy, he turned his mattress over and threw it and him against the wall to scare him. He was forced to leave Daddy's house. He then went to Mama Essie's house and threw himself on her bed. My mother had passed two years prior to this moment. Porjie cried loudly, "Mama, Mama, Mama!" My heart was jumping, but God allowed me to keep my composure, and my eyes were on Jesus.

Mama Essie told him (and I did also) over and over again, "You have to give yourself up and stop resisting arrest." He relaxed, and I began to thank God. Porjie gave himself up, but lo and behold, one of the officers said something terribly wrong to him, and he lost it. He kicked out the roof of the police car and some of the windows, causing the police to beat him. Later he told the judge that two of the officers kicked him as they were escorting him into the jail cell. Porjie also grabbed one of the officers in the wrong place. I told the judge that I heard someone at the restaurant admit they had tampered with his drink. The judge did believe me, and Porjie received a lesser sentence! He still had Mother's (Revelations 8:3–5) continuous prayers, and the Lord was with him right through hers and grandmother's too! He still got the beatings from Daddy (more jails and prisons)! Hallelujah! *Now*, you see one reason (chapter 6) I always hounded him to get saved! There were no Christian words of encouragement from Daddy to help Big Mama and Mama Essie in the *way* to go!

A word to the wise caretakers of these doubtful children! *We can* make a difference in comforting words of some kind of explanation.

Remember, I told you how Big Mama was so humble and quiet! Well, I thanked God many times for her sacrifice—her seed sowing and encouraging (Proverb 18:21) words for positive and fruitful living upon my daddy, Porjie, and all men—and *not* words of death upon them—so that they could possibly continue living especially unto their last days, praying, speaking for Daddy's life first, in leading the probable witnessing for the family. Big Mama said, "We just pray for your father that *he* is a good husband, a good father." And I, Esther, did love him dearly. Thank God *for that*! Since I grew up, *oh how* I do see much of the other way around this could have been! Now, don't you just see some of god's unconditional love building up in all His scepter touching anointed such times for me.

She said, "George did not know about nor felt he had to take the time to know how to deal with Porjie, thinking it all comes naturally. Men will nearly always be so much more different than women. This is revealed in my sold-out women's prison ministry right today. How God anointed us women before the foundation of this world to be His men's vision, praying, seed sowing, and Genesis 2:20B "help meet" to help these men meet their goals!

Big Mama continued, "Men mostly are impatient, intolerant, and are of no-nonsense mentality over certain behavior patterns!

Look to nobody's way but theirs!" Like Daddy went with it all till he truly believed in and received Jesus before passing on October 1983! Big Mama had also said how Daddy was definitely raised/trained in his Sunday school's teaching superintendent (Proverbs 22:6). Though he wanted to run from it, he couldn't hide! Hello, out there! In leading with all this dysfunction mentioned and with his antisocial, nonchalant self, he never bothered nobody! In his old-fashioned hard-working self, I know lots of you men can identify with him! Just take heed to Hebrew 13:5: "Remember, we do reap what we sow." He will help you and shall never leave nor forsake His own!

My siblings and I can thank Father God Almighty that, two weeks before Daddy passed, we all received a typewritten letter of sweet consolation from him, stating that *he does love us*! Hallelujah! He begged our forgiveness, and I had pumped into them to *always walk in* that kind of unconditional love of God, forgiving before he or anyone even asked for it (*beforehand*). Hallelujah!

He had been with some things within and just was not himself except for his carnal flesh! All I know is, he must have dealt with it before the eyes of God through the witness before somebody! For looking down at him in his casket, they could not shut/seal his mouth! And the Lord sealed with me that, yes, my daddy was finally free, happy with Jesus and He with him! Oh how I had looked at his pretty, shiny gold tooth and had kept staring at it, recalling my letting that fly go in his mouth many years earlier, but in repenting and asking for my Father God's unconditional love and Jesus's too, I was also free, *free*, *free*, *free*! Hallelujah! I was free without being able to muster up physical tears over him but just rejoicing that he made it in that day forevermore! I learned what true (Roman 14:17) righteousness, peace, and joy *in* the Holy Ghost down *on the inside* (unexplainable) really means! Hallelujah! This is what has kept me from criticizing others in *how they* praise and worship the Lord! Note: just since my marriage to *my Robert* (August 4, 1961), *I* learned to let it all hang out! Hallelujah!

Special Notation: In this God's timely book of precious memories, with most of its accounts truly hitting home in my heart, I bask in the Lord's will, for, His revelations has truly set me free in my mind! For the precious memories of my lovely mother, grandmothers, hardworking father, and grandfathers have been truly kept!

Precious Memories,
How they linger.
How they ever flood my soul.
In the stillness, of the midnight,
Sacred secrets He'll unfold!

—Author *Unknown*

It didn't matter whether I could or could not find anymore photographs, pictures, or snapshots of them when I went home recently. Margaret took pictures of me by the houses that were still standing. I just resolved that, like Charles Stanley says, "my precious family means more; in my heart, than any heirloom to me!" Time never changes His moments, His memories, His Love for them, the evening-time saints (in their humble sowings), for all eternity, and all of theirs gone on in joyful reaping nor me and all of mine to come and go, for:

My Times Are in Thy Hand!

"My God, I wish them there,
My life, my friends, my soul,
I leave entirely to Thy Care!
My times are in Thy Hand,
Whatever they may be
Pleasing or painful, dark or bright,
As best they seem to be!
My times are in Thy Hand,
Why, should I doubt or fear.
My Father's Hand will never cause
His child for a needless tear!"

This was derived from Psalms 31:15 and presented to our church choir by Lady Mother Ada K. Melvin here at St. Mark Church of Christ / Disciples of Christ, Goldsboro, North Carolina.

Chapter Eight

Favor Isn't Supposed to Be Fair

I said, "God, it isn't fair that I feel like I am walking around like a time bomb with all of Your living Word inside me. I feel like I have so much of Your favor in my life. I know that You want me to help somebody." The Holy Spirit encouraged me that being used for God's glory and favor isn't supposed to be fair when looking in the carnal flesh. I now understand why I was feeling spiritually full. Uncle Bill use to say, "We walk by faith and not by sight" (2 Corinthians 5:7).

William Henry Grady (Uncle Bill, my spiritual Mordecai) was an awesome man of God. He was dutiful, devoted, obedient, and faithful to the call in his life. He was a deacon, and his Holy Ghost anointing was powerful to his ministry. Uncle Bill was a wonderful man, a church devotee, and a community supporter. The favor of the Lord that was upon Uncle Bill poured into my life as well. I believe it was the Lord's sovereign will for Deacon William Henry Grady to step in and help his younger brother (my daddy) when we needed encouragement, especially the timid me, a teenage girl. Everybody was always praying for me after my mother passed away. My other siblings were not as vulnerable as I was.

Uncle Bill taught me the spiritual aspects of life and truly watched over me. I think of how Mordecai watched over Old Testament Esther as she was about to embark upon the most critical time of her life. She went to see the king (unannounced), which could have been very detrimental for Esther. In order for her Jewish nation to survive Haman's charge to have the Jews killed, a miracle needed to take place.

Both of my husbands were in the military. When I married my first husband, we had to move to his military duty station in New York (his hometown). Before my mother passed, I vowed that I would take care of her babies: my younger brother, Bobby (four years), and my sister, Laney (two years). I helped raise them when they were younger, and it was very difficult to make the decision to leave them in Indiana while I moved to New York with my first husband. I'll never forget my little brother, Bobby, who was nine years old at the time, sitting in the kitchen at Daddy's house with his blue pajamas on. He was dangling his feet the day I left and looking up at me. I don't know which one of us was more heartbroken. Well, he and Daddy bonded afterward, Big Mama kept Laney (she was seven years old), and Porjie was incarcerated again at the time.

Uncle Bill came to my rescue once again. He reminded me of my God-given wifely Genesis 2:20B "help meet" duties to help my husband meet his goal there is no distance in prayer. I knew that God would never leave me, so I moved to New York with peace of mind that I was doing the right thing. I was blessed with Uncle Bill's prayers for me and Grandma's blessings. The favor of God was truly over my family at all times. There is something about sowing the seed of encouraging words. These words can carry us through some very tough times. My marriage with my first husband did not work out. I left New York with my two sons Keith and Kevin and moved back to Indiana to stay with Mama Essie. She never breathed a mumbling word about what was going on until I was ready to volunteer about it.

My Uncle BillThe late deacon Willam H. Grady
& the late Aunt Anna Mae Grady

Years later, Uncle Bill and his lovely wife, Aunt Anna Mae, had been swindled out of some finances by a friend, which left them in a terrible grief. I was married to my second husband, Bob, at the time, and we were living in North Carolina. Bob agreed that I should go to Indiana and be with Uncle Bill and Aunt Anna Mae to see how I could be of assistance to them. They were overjoyed to see me. Aunt Anna Mae was not doing well and spent several days in the hospital. She stopped eating and even slipped into a coma. I remember the times I was sitting next to my mother while she was very ill in the hospital, but I knew she too could still hear me.

I continued to pray for and encourage Aunt Anna Mae, and I knew she could hear me too. Through the pain of seeing Aunt Anna Mae in a coma, I kept talking and sharing scriptures with her. All I could do was be there and speak the Word to her while fasting and praying. The favor of God allowed me to be in the ICU when I wasn't even supposed to be in there. I tell you, favor is fair in God's divine plan. Uncle Bill and I prayed together. He said something I shall never forget. He said, "The church is living in us, daughter. Acts 17:26. And the bound of how God's mind is made up is already set, and your Aunt Mae cannot be moved nor taken away from the Lord!"

I have never seen a heart defibrillator work, and they administered it to Aunt Anna Mae three times. After the last time, Uncle Bill knew that they couldn't revive her and made me fly back to North Carolina. I rejoiced in her departure because I knew she was going to be with the Lord. My Aunt Anna Mae was highly favored by God and was now home with Jesus. "To be absent from the body is to be present with the Lord!" (2 Corinthians 5:8).

I flew back to Indiana to attend Aunt Anna Mae's home-going celebration and surprised Uncle Bill. The favor of the Lord will always make a way for us. It sure enough was my "anointed such time" of the Lord to favor Uncle Bill! Little did I know that this would be the last time I would see Uncle Bill alive. Uncle Bill was a true man of God that understood his purpose on this earth. I think of him often to this day and thank God for everything that he taught me about Christian living.

When Uncle Bill was alive, he was such a blessing to my life and many others. When I was younger, he would give me his car to use anytime, and I never abused the privilege. He also allowed me the use of his car during my teenage and young adult years. On a serious note, my four-year-old son, Keith, almost ripped his finger off while playing with a rear storm door hinge. Uncle Bill allowed me to use his car to speed to Bunker Hill AFB Hospital, which was thirteen miles away. Uncle Bill held Keith's finger together with a man's pressure grip to stop the blood flow. Uncle Bill helped save Keith's finger. I was driving, and Uncle Bill was administering first aid. I may have lost it if I saw my child's finger in that condition. Maybe it was divine favor that our roles were reversed that day!

I remember another occasion while we were stationed at Andersen AFB, Guam, for three years (1971–1974). While we were in Guam, I had not been home to visit with my Indiana family for almost ten years. We were a military family that traveled extensively to duty stations all over the United States and on the Guam Island. Bob was struggling with guilt because I was away from my Indiana family for so long. Once we left the island, he unselfishly called Uncle Bill to see if he had permission to move me to North Carolina with the children. Although Bob always knew I would go with him anywhere, he still honored and respected Uncle Bill enough to ask his permission regarding our next place of residence. Uncle Bill always taught me to stand by my man and always support him. Interestingly enough, I did not know about Bob's call to Uncle Bill for years. My family and I ended up moving to North Carolina so we would be closer to Bob's family in Fayetteville, North Carolina, which was about fifty miles from Seymour Johnson AFB, in Goldsboro, North Carolina, where we were stationed. A word to young spouses: faithful obedience releases the favor of God. Hallelujah!

Uncle Bill saw Bob as a loving husband and father. Bob's character assured Uncle Bill that my children and I were in great hands. I have one vitally important comment that the book of Esther taught me. John 13:34–35B speaks of God's love that we should give one to another and become one with the Lord. In chapter 2 of Acts, Peter spoke the words of the prophet Joel regarding signs of the last days and occurrences. We cannot take our loving God's favor for granted. Mordecai reminded Esther of the spiritual logistics she had to take on then, and she immediately realized what needed to be done. For the church of our Living God, it is getting late in the evening, and the sun is eventually going to go down, but not the *son*—our eternally living Jesus Christ. We must make a conscious effort to live out our lives as the Lord purposed for each of us—to live with Him forever!

I must share a blessing I received as a military wife of a deceased, retired military spouse. From my husband, Bob's, 1978 air force retirement until his December 11, 2002, passing, he made a tremendous sacrifice—by adding more finances into his military survivor's benefit plan (SBP) for me. Our family would always surprise each other any way we could, and this one topped them all! All that the Defense Finance Accounting System (DFAS) knew and stated was that Bob overpaid his account premiums. I did see the document, and he had checked on it all just the day before he passed—on December 10, 2002. I was unaware of the financial increase until three and a half years after he passed. God is an on-time God with His fair sovereign favor, and I give Him all the glory, honor, and praise!

In 1967 since returning from Vietnam, he was able to submit a claim due to the symptoms he received from the chemical called Agent Orange. Agent Orange was used to clear away the foliage that hindered the war zone mission. I walked into the Office of the Military Widow's Affairs to check on the Agent Orange claim. His illness was that it was Agent Orange related. Thank the Lord; he kept up the fight!

Bob stated that someday the military may have to give the compensation to all the soldiers who were exposed to the Agent Orange that was in the air. While I was in the same office, someone said, "You do not have your cost refund, do you?" I was completely unaware of what he was talking about, but he kept probing, and I did too. Only a couple of weeks went by, and I was favored to be put in a new and different status, "Purpose well served. All debts cleared!" God is an on-time God. Yes, He is! Many thanks for our fair-favoring Lord God for my receiving the blessed compensation that Bob had planned for his family. I thank the Lord for his favor that blessed Bob and his family.

If you are a military widow, please check or recheck to see if there are benefits that you are entitled to that you may not be aware of. Please contact DFAS and inquire of all insurance premiums that you should have received. You owe it to your family to find out how much you are entitled to from the SBP and whether these premiums were initially set up. Thank you, Bob, for all that you provided for me and the children. The favor of God ain't supposed to be fair to those who may not understand, but it is certainly appreciated.

You really have to be a child of God to take the bad with the good. Both women and men must show unconditional love for one another. As I mentioned before, initially I was not able to speak about Jesus or read the Bible in our home. Robert was not against the Lord, but during this time in his life, he could not see how the enemy was trying to manipulate our relationship. I also believe that Satan tried to use him to intimidate me at times. I knew that the battle was the Lord's and that we must let God do His mighty works in and through us. God allows us to know the battle is just right for Him. If we totally take our hands off everything and let God handle it. We can have peace in the midst of any storm. If we truly let God fight our battles, His divine favor will fall on us. God allows us to be tested to simply show that He is God. We must keep our spiritual eyes on Jesus and not on our spouses. My initial sermon was "What Price the Anointing? It Costs Something." We need the divine favor of God to prevail in our minds and in our hearts. We must also continue to seek His face and loving arms of protection.

I recall coming home one night from a powerful revival service at St. Mark. We received a very explosive message of the Lord delivered by Apostle Norbert Simmons of Deeper Life Church Ministries of Goldsboro, North Carolina, such as his members said he had never preached before! His sermon left me knowing without the shadow of a doubt that I now know what "wearing the anointing" means! For the first time ever, Bob met me at the door that evening as if I didn't have my own key. Although the amazing message was still with me, I never said a mumbling word. The Lord revealed to me later how His anointing in and all over me overpowered the enemy that was given place that night (Ephesians 4:27). No wonder in his spewing out,

Bob became very irate as I have never seen him before! As clearly as I remember his words today, he said, "Don't be bringing all that mess up in here. Just go back and let your church take care of you!" He then took off, saying, "I'm going in the back to get my gun!"

Now, my sisters and brothers, this was not the time for me to get all mixed up with opinions. The Lord quickly revealed to me what I should do. If I said anything, it would have been a lost cause, so I chose to pray instead. I went to my daughter Margaret's house (five minutes away) while she was speaking with Bob on the phone. I did not know what she and her father talked about, but I knew that God was working it out. I immediately conversed with God and asked, "Lord, You want me to go back up in there?" He said, "Yes," and my faith was increased even. The Lord was my encouragement, whereas Mordecai was Esther's chief encourager. I was determined to stand still and see the salvation of the Lord (Exodus 14:13) that it was already done. Certainly, it was all up in this Esther's "anointed such time," touching of the scepter of God!

My dear sisters and brothers, please pause with me. Hopefully, I haven't lost you as I am becoming freer while writing each chapter. I pray as I am revisiting the details of what happened that night that one soul out there may also be freed. It was incredible how the enemy tried to show his true colors that night through my husband. The enemy has a way of always trying to throw a curveball from out of nowhere. It reminds me of another situation; just talking about it is a major test in my life.

In 1975 we had just moved into our newly built home in Goldsboro, North Carolina. As we know, when a new home is built, insects, animals, or other things have a tendency to either stick around or flee. As I was happily working in my flower bed (along the front of the house), I saw something move from the corner of my eye. It was a snake, a creepy crawling critter that I despise looking at or even talking about. My husband, children, and anyone that knows me will validate my fear of these things to the point that I can't even call them what they are by name!

It had the nerve to move upward along the crevice between the porch and the sidewalk. I totally despise these reptiles to the point that I don't even like for them to be mentioned around me. After the flower bed incident that day, I recall crying and telling Bob that I was going back home (Indiana). He replied, "Well, shame on you." I knew that I could not allow something so horrific to chase me away from my home.

I was going to keep my eyes on the Lord and let Him fight this battle for me. If the Lord was able to help me be delivered through my flower bed incident (as significant as that was), He certainly can guide my hand and walk through this season in my life with my husband. I have to admit every now and then I still look over at the corner of the house and even though my friends and family members encouraged me to believe that it will never come back again. The truth sets us free (John 8:32, 36). As I sat in my daughter's house, I was praying and waiting to hear from the Lord.

I kept pondering in my heart about the Word. The Word revealed in my life has given me courage above all things. I had to continue to believe that God had purposed me for so much more in my life and that He's not finished with me by a long shot. At this moment in time, I had to be able to feel the Holy Spirit; the very presence of His "such time" of anointing that is in me was so that I can make the right decisions in my life. I never felt in my heart that Bob would have harmed me in any way. He just needed some time to think it over. After I prayed to God for the right answer over my life, I arose and returned home. The Lord's response to me may not be the same for others, but it was important for me to have faith and to walk in it. His scepter touching for this Esther spirit of "anointed such time" had me curling up in the same bed and going to sleep in peace! Yes, it had to be Jesus!

I heard the Holy Spirit lead and guide me. I also heard the prayers of my Uncle Bill, my grandmothers, Bishop Smith, and my late pastor, Bishop James L. Melvin, said, "Devil, you're a liar." The Lord was saying, "It's proving time now." After all the messages that were ministered and all the songs that were sung (like "Take the Name of Jesus with You Everywhere You Go"), it was time to be tested. He said, "Prove me now that My name will be highly exalted over every situation." I yelled that the devil was a liar and rebuked him. I yelled so loud on my way home but never said a mumbling word to Bob about my release in the car when I got home. It was forever sold out to Jesus Christ. The favor of the Lord was within me, this modern-day Esther spirit, never leaving nor forsaking me (Hebrews 13:5b). I do let brotherly love continue (Hebrews 13:1)—all for the fair-favored, inward Holy Spirit moving from such spiritually anointed scepter touching in this "such time"!

Bob was not saved at the time, but he was God's child. He had to see God's sovereign favor over his life too. I continued to love Bob unconditionally for better or for worse and in sickness and in health. Speaking of health, not too long after this incident, Bob was unable to breathe well for three full months. When he could not sleep, I sat up with him at home and in the hospital as well. He had a sleep apnea test, and I stayed with him until he fell asleep (the hospital made me leave). For three months, he pulled back the curtains at night or went out on the porch because he couldn't sleep. Bob always felt smothered due to lack of sleep. I was so grateful that his breathing was back to normal and he was feeling better at the end of the third month. My prayers for my husband were truly answered once again. For better or worse, I loved him dearly and vowed to always be there for him unconditionally.

I was favored that night as I returned to the house. I continued to support Bob's needs and loved him through everything. I knew he also had a purpose and he would eventually line up and fulfill the purpose God had for him. Therefore, I did not need to interfere with the anointing over his life. I just wanted to see the fulfillment of Christ being present in his life.

Since the Old Testament, God has anointed His men for their authoritative leading of whatever their predestination was going to be. We are required to pray for our "kings and priests." 1 Timothy 2:1 says that God has blessed us so that we all may lead a quiet and peaceful life in all godliness and honesty. Ladies, as I shared before, prayer is very beneficial for us. We must also pray for our men, which will let them know that they are being supported by us. The support that is provided will not only benefit them but will also benefit the entire family. I don't know about you, but I do not intend to allow God's

Word to return void.[16] God's Word must spring forward throughout all generations. I was blessed to receive a message regarding "the balance act" at the 2005 Hampton University Minister's Conference. I know life is a balancing act, and we must balance all aspects of our lives so we can serve God's people more effectively.

Now some of you might have the following questions:

1. How was she able to deal with all of the things that occurred?

   Yes, we see many things in the flesh in this life as impossible, but we are told in Luke 1:37, "For, with God, nothing shall be impossible." God has given us the Holy Spirit to help empower us, to comfort us, and to lead us into victory. Because we truly love Him, we are able to walk in our (purposed) calling while believing and receiving God's promises. We know that all things are working together for our good in His own way, at His own will, and in His own time!
2. Why did she put up with it all?

   First of all, it was and will always be God that will get the glory for everything that I have endured by, with, and through Christ Jesus in me (John 12:23–28). Philippians 2:5 says, "Let this mind be in you, which was also in Christ Jesus," and His 2 Corinthians 12:9 strength is made perfect in our weakness proving the anointing power He promised, "My grace is sufficient for thee." God's favor is not understood by the carnal mind; we would misuse and abuse it. When we stay carnal-minded, we are not able to let God have His way. I am striving to seek first the kingdom of God daily, so I can receive His promise of "peace that surpasses all understanding."[17]
3. Some may also say, "I don't think I would have . . ."

---

16 Isaiah 55:11.

17 Philippians 4:7.

I can only pray we prepare for more of the Lord's walking in Acts of obedience for us unto overcoming the hinderant accusing of the devil's attacks upon the brethren in each of us and ours. (Revelation 12:11) Overcoming the devil (or Satan)/freeing from eternal damnation with him! Victory!!!:

A. by the blood of the precious Lamb of God,
B. by the sold-out word of our testimony and being sold out as witnesses of obedience in Jesus Christ before others, and
C. by not being ashamed of the Gospel of Christ (Romans 1:16).

Favor isn't supposed to be fair, but when God releases it, we are allowed in our belief to receive it and walk in it in our "Esther spirit anointed such time" needed in touching the spiritual scepter of God! It is such a relief to know we can live by God's free and unmerited favor with Him forever. Now *that's* favor! Amen.

Chapter Nine

Accepting What God Allows: Who Am I to Second-Guess Our Sovereign God?

Whatever God can use in my life to bless others, then I count it all as *joy* in the Holy Ghost[18] all for His kingdom. We are God's laborers and his fellow workers in the body of Christ.[19]

Mordecai encouraged Esther to allow herself to be used by God, which saved the Jews. Queen Esther was sold out for God. Acts 17:28 says, "For in Him, [Christ Jesus, by the Holy Ghost's Spirit] we live and move and have our being.[20] We are to accept what God allows in our commitment to Him. God will truly bless those who bless you.[21] Everyone should have a burning desire to pray for peace. We need to have peace between our very walls.[22] John 14:27 says, "Peace I [Christ Jesus] leave with you, my peace I give to you, not as the world gives do I give to you. Let not your hearts be troubled, neither let it be afraid." We truly need peace in our homes and in our lives on a daily basis. The Lord's peace is to comfort us in continuous prayer for Jerusalem's peace, especially His beloved, for His sake (Psalms 122:6) through us!

Esther set the example of representing the church within the church of our Living God. It was an inside job. I highly recommend that we do not take Mordecai (a representation of the Holy Spirit) for granted. Mordecai causes us to think of everything that was in

18 James 1:2.

19 1 Corinthians 3:9–10; Ephesians 4:12–16.

20 Acts 17:28.

21 Genesis 12:3.

22 Psalm 122:7.

jeopardy regarding the Jewish nation, the lineage of Jesus Christ of forty-two generations. As I share my heart, I am well able to accept what God allows as Mordecai and Esther chose to do. I believe it is conducive to the kingdom of God and His Word shall not return void.

Our granddaughter Samantha Mary Perara w/ father Master Sergeant Bryan L. Avey

Allow me to share a touching experience about our granddaughter Samantha. She was raised up in church since she was a newborn baby. When she was around the age of six or seven, she became very sensitive at the mentioning of Jesus dying on the cross. She was told how Jesus died so we could be free from our sins forevermore. Her father, Bryan, took her fishing one day. When they came home, she was quite excited about all the fish they caught. They were getting ready to prepare the fish for frying and eating. It was Bryan's first time cleaning them, and Samantha was unaware of the true bravery he displayed. Lo and behold, he began cutting it at the neck, and the blood spurted out. It was the shock of Samantha's lifetime, for she was utterly saying over and over, "I wasn't ready!" You can imagine how hurt for her he was as well!

I tried to calm her down over the telephone by sharing a story with her. I said, "Samantha, we love you, sugar, and God and Jesus love you, even your real tears. Always remember, God says everything on this earth has a purpose. The fish has a purpose. The Bible says that even Jesus ate fish, and it's good for us too. But the blood that kept the fish alive had to go so the fish could be prepared to be able to nourish our bodies. Okay? God bless you."

As Samantha calmed down, I used a different approach. I told Sammy, "When I was a little girl like you, our pastor would come over to our house to eat, and he loved to eat chicken. He would say, 'The chicken died that I might live, for the chicken had a purpose.' God allowed the fish and the chicken to die so we may eat it. It was a sacrifice for them, but we would starve to death if we didn't eat the things that God allowed." She was able to understand the stories that I shared with her regarding the preparation process and the sacrifices that are necessary for God's people. She understood the things that God allowed, which made her feel better.

The story of sacrifice I shared with Samantha reminds me of the sacrifice Jesus made for us. We can identify with His precious blood that was shed on the cross at Calvary. Christ (who was without sin) died for us. His blood was shed for all our sins, present and future, to remind us of the sacrifice He made for His people. We must continue to accept what God allows, even if we may not fully understand the process.

God desires for us to live without sin. If we are obedient on earth, we will be able to live forevermore with Jesus when He returns for us. Mordecai said, "Yet who knows whether you have come to the kingdom for such a time as this?"[23] His word to Esther was a time of obedience and spiritual growth for both of them. The actual part of spiritual growth in the principles of the kingdom of God is the most serious thing we need to learn. It is God whom we are to focus on and through Christ Jesus, and the provisions of His teachings cannot

[23] Esther 4:14.

be taken lightly. Mordecai and Esther went into deep intimacy with God by praying and fasting against Haman's plot." They would not have known to pray and fast if they weren't already connected with the Lord and His Word.

Esther, for many of us, represents the living prophetic church within the church today. We, the true Church within, should pull together to be on one accord in resolving similar matters that today each church has to face. The natural man must become a born-again spiritual man before we are capable of receiving and understanding the spiritual things of God.[24] As a spiritual man, we should be able to accept what God allows and not second-guess His decisions for us.

The Holy Spirit is waiting to help us build up His love, trust, and respect in and toward one another by:

A. building on our faith in the things of God and believing that He will provide for us,
B. obeying the Word of the Lord and producing the Fruit of the Spirit that is pleasing to Him,[25] and
C. assembling together as God works in the midst of us.

We are to exhort one another, for the Bible says for us to be there for one another.

Exhorting means "to encourage, press, push, urge" unto the mutual edification, building up the body of Christ Jesus from within and not of ourselves. The heart of Esther was to save the Jewish people. Jesus' heart is to save the world from our sins. It is to our benefit to allow Christ to have free reign in our lives. Esther allowed the Lord to search her heart so she could do the right thing. Mordecai's job was to encourage her and provide to her a sense of urgency for what she needed to do. The cry of God is for us to accept what He allows in His only begotten Son, Jesus, throughout all generations. We must be able to hear from Him and allow His will to perfect what is in us for His glory.

---

[24] 1 Corinthians 2:14.

[25] Galatians 5:22, 23.

We need to love one another as Christ loves us. Can you imagine if Mordecai loved only himself? Can you imagine if Esther only loved herself? We need to encourage one another and establish a positive role in another person's life other than our own. It is for our benefit to live a holy life. God desires that, with His unconditional love, we are to promote unity in our ministries. We need to exhort one another as (Genesis 4:9) true brothers and sisters would keep watch over one another. Let's get back to true fellowship and relationship with the people of God.

God is very serious about people business. We cannot fake on God, and we certainly don't want Him to fake on us! Jesus told Nicodemus, "Most assuredly, I say to you, unless one is born again, he cannot see the Kingdom of God" (John 3:3). Although Mordecai and Esther did not have the Holy Spirit's indwelling and empowerment provision like we have today, their hearts and the heart of the Jews sought the Lord's help and received it. God's name was not mentioned in the book of Esther, but her faith was activated in the Lord hands down. Where do we stand today in our kingdom walk and trust in the Lord?

As I walk into my destiny, I will forever trust that Jesus is cheering me on. I know in my heart that He is literally rooting for all of us to make it to heaven when our day has ended on earth. I preached a New Year's message one night entitled "Just Jesus." His name is *the* choice in every aspect of our lives. We can call upon *the* name morning, noon, or night and know that Jesus will hear us. Whatever needs that we are faced with at any moment, we can simply petition them before Christ and know that all our prayers will be answered according to His will, His way, and in His own time.

I pray, "Lord, that we will always keep Your message and Your Word before us and in us. We are in this Christian walk together, so we ask that you prepare us to have the strength and desire to support one another." Amen. Christ is the only way, truth, and the life (John 14:6). Galatians 5:16 commands us to walk in the spirit. Walk in His Spirit, and we shall not fulfill the lust of the worldly fleshy ways. I encourage all of us to believe, receive, and walk in the anointing and power of the Holy Spirit. I'm believing for kingdom results of God's divine favor. Mordecai shared something with Esther that was important to her. Esther was not only the queen; she also had a Jewish nation to be concerned about. Esther accepted what God allowed, and her nation was freed. She was willing to accept the challenge at any cost. Are we willing to accept the things that God has laid before us to endure for the purpose of His sovereign kingdom?

God allows us to forgive others and forgive ourselves. When we open the door of forgiveness, we are no longer bound by tricks of the enemy. While Jesus was on the cross, he said in Luke 23:34, "Father, forgive them for they know not what they do." Saints of God, I pray each morning that God makes me an earthen vessel of His inward peace and unconditional love, which is my primary and lasting passion in ministry. To God be the glory for *all* that He has done for me. I choose to accept what God allows, and if I perish, then I will perish. I have and will allow God to use me. I will not allow a Haman spirit to hinder God's great works in my life. I thank the Lord for direct access to Christ. We don't have to ask anyone if we can have a conversation or spend time with Jesus. Now that's something to talk about!

I have been assigned to three men's prison ministries and now to two women's prisons. I do not take the required compassion for prison ministry lightly. For 1 John 3:17 speaks about our God's loving BOCs (bowels of compassion) to certainly be flowing in every successful mission therein! Truly, it's a mission of us Esther spirits in the Holy Spirit of Christ anointing that's needed more than ever before. In every such time for the power of God in spiritual-scepter touching, God does provide (Philippians 4:19).

When we walk into the prisons, we must be patient and caring as they share their circumstances with us. These inmates we call residents (even in our maximum-security prisons) must be able to feel comfortable for us to win their trust so they can share what God has laid or even not laid on their hearts! In this listening ministry, though called Yokefellow with us ministers going in praying they become Isaiah 10:27 vs. Yoked with Jesus together with us we're there to simply offer them Christ—His way and at His will—as they see Him in us in relationship and in His unconditional love before it is eternally too late!

Jesus could have very easily petitioned to God to have the thief (that was on the cross next to Him) be taken off the cross, but He did not allow that to happen for a reason. The thief was still entitled to walk out of his punishment. When the thief asked Jesus to remember him in paradise, he believed that He was the Son of God. Jesus ultimately granted the request and stated that he would be remembered in paradise (Luke 23:39–43). Nowadays, let us just band together more, praying and seeking for more expedient DNA justifications for the wrongly accused. Meanwhile, we all are to be ready for that great day *whenever* it is. There is a song that says, "Who shall be able to stand?"

Saints, we should all come to accept what God allows. The thief who was received in heaven with Christ believed in Him. Sin comes with a price, but God is a loving God, and He desires for everyone to receive salvation through His Son, Jesus Christ. There are many things that God allows that would make us scratch our heads in amazement. In our prison ministry, every inmate in the death row with capital punishment can have the opportunity to receive Christ before leaving this earth. As Jesus accepted the thief into paradise, it is our responsibility to accept the inmate's salvation, also having become our brother and our sister, which is also through Jesus Christ, not forgetting this is their "Esther spirit anointed time, touching the spiritual-scepter of God."

The anointing is to flow to all of us from heart to heart, lifting the name of Jesus Christ. "Judgment must begin at the house of God." First Peter 4:17 says, "For the time has come for judgment to begin at the house of God, and if it begins with us first, what will be the end of those who do not obey the gospel of God?" As Christians, other people should be able to see Christ in us, and His Anointing should be a reflection of our lives. They should be able to see the obedience of a worshipful lifestyle for the Lord in us.

I believe that the Lord is preparing us for true street ministry. Why would we want someone to accept our God that is in us and live as we live when we are failing to live our lives for God the way we are supposed to? What kind of example are we living? God will allow us to make mistakes because there is teaching and learning principles in the mistakes we make. However, Mark 9:42 says, "But whosoever causes one of these little ones who believe in Me to stumble, it would be better for him if a millstone were hung about his neck and he were thrown into the sea." Wow, isn't that something?

The "little ones" the Bible is speaking of is not only our little children. The little ones also mean the 'babes (people who are new to their salvation) in Christ. We can easily lead them astray by turning them off and away from living a life with Christ. We certainly do not want a Haman spirit to turn one of God's own away from the Lord. Let's focus on not being so judgmental about what's right and wrong and put all of our focus on who we can lead to salvation in Christ *today*! If someone is not preaching or teaching the gospel in a godly way, woe to them that have to answer to the Lord! Therefore, it is not our job to judge those that are not properly leading the Lord's people, but it is our job each of being accountable to ensure that the children of God are being properly fed, trained, and equipped for the kingdom.

We are also standing in the gap for the pastors, elders, and ministers that are speaking the truth—the infallible (never-lying), the immutable (never-changing), and the incorruptible (never-decaying) living Word of God to us and in us. We love you, trust you, and salute your commitment to the obedience of God's work as you release your time and gifts to His kingdom. Thank you for your sacrifice and dedication to serve the Lord and His people. Thank you for all the midnight oil that you have burned in preparing to take the children of God where He wants us to be.

We cannot allow the enemy to have a foothold in our lives. God loves us, and we are to trust and believe in Him as His master plan will be fulfilled according to the scriptures. Can you imagine Esther and the Jewish nation's continued support from God after Haman's death (Hebrews 13:8)? Do we believe that God is in our present and future as He was in the past? God's beloved Jews are very present and will have a strong future because of one powerful decision Esther made. She heard from God through Mordecai. I heard through Uncle Bill!

Esther's Jewish family grew against Haman's determination to see them destroyed. Obviously, Esther was *about family*. In chapter 9 of the book of Esther, the Feast of Purim enjoined these ordained memorial days for the Jewish family throughout all generations. They were to celebrate for two days every year to remind them that their nation was saved in the days of Esther. In keeping with God's covenant through Abraham in Genesis 12:3, God declares, "I will bless those who bless you, and I will curse him who curses you; and in you all families of the earth shall be blessed." Abraham was given the blessings to live on forevermore.

Esther was a very courageous woman. She walked in her purpose, which she was called to. I have to share a courageous story of my own regarding acceptance. My grandfather, Daddy Bob, made me sit in back of his station wagon on one of the scariest missions of my life. He knew I was deathly afraid of dogs. When I was approximately six years old, I knew there was a God somewhere, considering the fact that all of us were raised up in the church. We drove out to the country on this particular day. My horrible task was to release our beautiful *white* dog, Snowball, out to be seen no more.

My emotions were all mixed up as a child, and I didn't understand what was going on. I was glad that I didn't have to be afraid of our dog anymore, but I was very sorrowful that something might happen to Snowball. I still had to find love in my heart for Daddy Bob after what happened, but I shall never forget this experience. I just thank God for the chance since of being saved, knowing the significance of why I had to repent over Snowball and *Ebony*, which you are about to hear about. Even though I am crying as I write this, I know I am freed. Hallelujah! My grandmother Mama Essie told me something which is more meaningful to me now. She said, "Snowball had a purpose on this earth too. Everything that belongs to God has a purpose."

I recall that several years ago, before my husband passed, Bob made me do the same thing with our black dog, Ebony. Well, our dogs were not prejudiced, and neither were we. While our children were being raised, my husband and my children were unaware of my fear of dogs. God has interesting ways about everything. Romans

4:17 says, "Calling those things which do not exist as though they did." The Lord gave our family solace in knowing that both dogs received a good home. Someday we will all join them again in glory!

One year I visited my daughter Margaret at Dyess Air Force Base in Texas. Like the old saying goes, "I'll be dog bite my behind," if Margaret and her roommate didn't leave their young black-and-white Australian sheep border collie with me while they were at work. I nearly died and was scared half to death! The thing that you do for your children without them knowing your concerns is incredible! Her dog was a long, tall, skinny, and very energetic mixed sheep-herder, and her name was JJ.

JJ darted back and forth and around me all day long until they came back home. I really thought I would just die. I never showed my fear to the dog, but with what I now know about dogs, JJ already knew my fears! I tell you, she kept trying my patience. I remember my parents sharing a story about a certain dog that jumped in my carriage (when I was a baby) while my mother walked me down the street. The story was highly disturbing, and I know it affected me.

Years later, as only God would have it, JJ stole and melted my heart. We became great buddies, and she was even considered as one of my granddaughters. It had to be Jesus that worked out our relationship. It seemed that every time Margaret needed to go on a one-year tour in the military, she would ask Bob and me to keep JJ, which was a treat for us and for our dog. I can honestly say, she was such a beautiful black-and-white dog, and she made up for Snowball (our white dog) and for Ebony (our black dog). I believe JJ represented them both in a loving way when she came into my life (for Esther's anointed times at their best) and for the prevailed touching of the Spiritual Scepter of God!

Our late beautiful dag "J.J" w/ Robert @ her soothing bath time!

Our granddaughter Samantha w/ her mother, our daughter,
U.S. of America Air Force retired Msgt. Margaret E. Perara

I was blessed from accepting what God allows. When JJ's breed made "Dog of the Year" (during the Babe movie season), she looked prettier than any dog I had ever seen. We should have entered her in contests. One of the saddest days I can ever remember was the day we lost JJ. While Margaret and my granddaughter Samantha were living on Langley AFB, Virginia, Margaret had to put JJ to sleep due to old age. She was fifteen human years old and one of the sweetest dogs that ever to existed. I can only imagine how it really affected them—my daughter and granddaughter in Virginia. We all finally accepted what God allowed. I am sure there are others out there who can identify with the love for an animal. We felt we lost a granddaughter that day, but we know she is running and darting around paradise all day with Bob. Our nine-year-old granddaughter, Samantha, found it harder to accept what God allowed as she and JJ literally grew up together. She talks about her often and was attached to JJ much sooner than I did when I first met her! ☺

One of my friends from Kokomo Indiana (Nancy) passed away and was unable to attend our fiftieth class reunion. I had told her over the telephone one year that I was going to bring the silver orchid earrings I had borrowed from her fifty years prior to our reunion. Another friend's (Joan Townsend Runels) husband was stationed with Nancy's husband, which rarely ever happens. Joan had taken very good care of Nancy in her last days of fighting cancer. I had a little time of dealing with the loss and not being able to see her at the reunion. I understood that God had a plan for Nancy and was grateful for Joan's ministry to her.

When I went home, I surprised Joan (who didn't have anything to remember Nancy by) by giving her the earrings I was going to give Nancy. It overwhelmed Joan more than I thought (which truly blessed me). I was finally able to accept what God allowed for Nancy. The gesture also brought tears to the rest of my beautiful, blessed classmates: Janet Beard and her sister Sarah Jane, Mary "Trixie" Schoolfield, my aunt Mildred (and her husband, Willie Lewis), Connie Waters, Eddie Pearl Haile, Daisy Bonnafon, Dorothy Stevenson (and her husband, William), and Reba Harris (and her husband, Oscar). The night we shared was a lasting milestone of a marvelous time we had. My daughter Margaret was a hit with them too and was told that she resembled me a lot when I was younger in the 1950s.

I returned to North Carolina after the reunion ended. I was so eager to get home that I left my cell phone on the plane. I did not realize what I did until I ran into a very nice valet on the way to my car. While I was in the airline valet wheelchair, he ended up searching for the phone in the lost-and-found office. I thought all was lost, but he was able to find my phone. I thanked him and left the airport.

I started down the highway and drove up to approximately six or seven State Trooper vehicles. I looked over to the right, and there was a terrible accident. A red station wagon was so badly mangled and wrapped around a tree that it was unrecognizable. All I could do was pray for all those involved. Then I thought that it could have been me. I had accepted what God allowed regarding the search for my cell phone, which delayed my travel home. I arrived home, well rested and thanking the Lord that I was alive but also so sorrowful and prayerful for all of those involved!

When I got home from the airport, I felt the Lord was telling me to write the book. I have lived in North Carolina for over thirty years. I often wondered if I should get away from the area to begin the journey (even to the mountains somewhere) of writing about my life and my family experiences. I knew after seeing the accident and hearing from the Lord that it was time to write the book. Above all things, yes, I received gout in my knee, but it didn't have me. I used the time of rest to immediately start on the book while I was laid up in the house. The Lord put my busy life on hold, and I had to accept what God allowed, saying, "Well, Lord, I got my mountain. Nevertheless, I thank you for the opportunity!" Therefore, I must be obedient in doing what is necessary to help others to His glory.

The late Bishop James L. Melvin and Lady Mother Ada K. Melvin

For twenty-seven years, I was very blessed to hear many anointed messages and have taken dictation of every word from a very special life-changing messenger of the Lord—my late pastor, Bishop James L. Melvin. One special message that just continue to ring in my spirit even today is entitled, "Trust in the Lord, He's Working It out Right Now!" The sub was "Whatever He Hasn't Worked out, He's Working on It!" For God is working it all together for His sovereign good for us! I trust and respect that He is the Lord of my purposed life. Bishop Melvin's beautiful wife, Lady Mother Ada K. Melvin says, "We cannot go out of here on a flowery bed of ease any more than Jesus did at Calvary until we have done as our Master pleases."

I know that Christ shall never leave nor forsake me (Hebrews 13:5b). Over the years, I have resolved the fact that it is the only way I can live. Bishop Melvin would always say, "The church is always alive and doing well." We must remember that we should "not grow weary while doing well, for in due season, we shall reap if we do not lose heart."[26] We must continue to do well in our lives and accept what God allows in our daily walk with Him. For how can we miss

[26] Galatians 6:9.

in our Esther spirit of Christ's "anointed such times, touching the scepter of God"?

We must accept what God allows, yes, even though this recent five months of tonsil cancer, beyond my control, has grabbed me so! Certainly, it's God's sovereignty! How dare I allow myself to get stuck in this manuscript's last phase of writing/finalizing all this time!

Now I see how my Lord's true purpose has come alive in my spirit amid this most devastating stage IV tonsil cancer (God's sovereignty)! I met my daughter's beautiful friend, Barbara Short, while I was in northern Virginia, one of the best facilitated areas of cancer treatment! She was so bravely, diligently, and faithfully completing the typing I needed before I return to North Carolina (God's sovereignty)! She is also in her very own identifiable stage of cancer!

Bringing up the rear a bit, in as much as my *last but best* chapter of this book is about my husband, Robert, I could not resist my Lord's encouragement about how I cannot stop now trusting in His master plan! It's all in my coming by faith and belief for my 120 years of life that I asked for if it is the Lord's will and beyond my asking! I pray that others out there, touching the anointed scepter of God, can recall such needy time of this old faith song with me, "When all around my soul gives away, He is my solid rock anchor, my hope, my stay! Yes, Lord, Your anointing power doeth hold within the vale!"

As I continue the 1 Corinthians 15:31 of "dying daily" of this carnal fleshy hindrance on this side of glory. In my treatments I kept remembering 1 Thessalonians 5:18 (in everything, giving thanks!) against every yoke of stronghold that is around my spiritual neck (Isaiah 10:27). I did not tell anybody what to do but how I came through, how I got over it, and not what they are to be expected to have to go through, even as I blamed tonsil cancer on the husk of popcorn kernel that had gotten lodged in my throat and with most doctors saying, "No." Most likely, it may have brought the timely and proper attention to things (God's sovereignty). Yes, it was at God's very own timely "such time!" Mind you, I am from Indiana and was raised up on corn/popcorn! Also, have you ever heard of tonsils growing back again? Mine were removed when I was a little girl. Yes, I know it's quite a controversy! *But God!*

This all continued last fall, September 8, 2011, when my most efficient primary Goldsboro, North Carolina, doctor—Muhammed A. Bhatti, MD—sent me a biopsy result by EENT Dr. Michael Johnson, Goldsboro, North Carolina. Whereas with the confirmation of my stage IV tonsil cancer, I in turn pointed up to God faithfully saying, "He has it now I don't." My daughter Margaret lives in Haymarket, Virginia, where my most likely best care was to be given. Like I said in a highly favorable area of my needy cancer treatment, the ball began rolling! I was so beautifully catered to by Dr. Richard Gardner (Prince William Hospital, Manassas, Virginia); Dr. Bruce Davidson (Georgetown University Hospital and president of the Head & Neck Department, Washington, DC); Dr. David M. Heyer and Jessica Tsai, PA-C (Oncology and Hematology, Fairfax/Reston, Virginia), administrators of five once-a-week cisplatin chemotherapy treatment; and also by Dr. Jefferson E. C. Moulds, administrator of my thirty-three consecutive days of every day x-rays and radiation (Reston Hospital, Reston, Virginia).

Continuing down now, I had one week left for preparing there to take care of myself back in North Carolina! No problem. I'd continue my medicine regimen and the flushing of my kidneys with plenty of water, which was the main thing right now! Lots of rest. Isn't it amazing how I am just now being aware of this timely prophetic resting spot for me—Reston hospital, Virginia? I had nothing to do but rest-on in my needy dilemma. I shall continue. Once back in North Carolina, I was to better exercise practices toward a more-effective evangelism.

Just remember, I cannot tell you what to do. Each of us is different. We have different physicians, and we react differently to treatments. I didn't even lose any hair, and my fingernails grew! Hallelujah! I just can't find the right things to eat or suit my fancy—believe it or not! I have been known to be a good eater, and I lost sixty pounds! The Zofran (for nausea and vomiting) is just about to conquer it all! Yes, I know, it all is conquered in the Romans 8:37 spirit and in the Revelations 12:11 spirit! It's already done—in the Spirit—at Calvary! Right? By it alone, all Esther spirits have our anointed such times! Amen.

Got to *report*!

By the Holy Ghost's anointed power of our God by, with, and through what Christ Jesus invested within me, I—His trusting, believing, sold-out-to-Him, and greatly committed servant—come to you after this three-year journey so far. I'm back home again in good ole North Carolina in October 2015! I decree and proclaim to you that I'm totally healed, delivered, and set free from that dreadful ole Haman spirit stage IV tonsil cancer! Hallelujah!

I was running on in missions after mission of work in my (Nehemiah 8:10) "joy of the Lord" strength in Him, still walking by Faith and not by carnal flesh or negative sight! I believe and keep a tunnel-vision focus on Jesus alone. And it's the same Romans 8:37 conquering for my sisters and brothers out there for your anointed scepter touching and agreeing in your "such times"!

"Another precise report: December 30, 2016 going into the New Year of 2017, and my fifth year journey bring "Cancer Free", my pastor and my church (St. Mark Church of Christ disciples of Christ, Goldsboro allows me to head a Cancer Support Group. Praise God!

I am just blessed-to-be-a-blessing! Last, but not the least, is two of the most dreadful/toughest needy times for the help of our Lord's Holy Ghost power of anointing in our Perara family's life for me!

My son Kevin Dwayne Perara Sr. (who lived in Milwaukee Wisconsin), his car was totaled being hit head-on by an 18-wheeler truck! The doctor at Freodert Hospital (the one and same hospital in the heavily-needed weekend of the many needy Sikh Temple massacre patients!), called me here in Goldsboro N.C. saying, "every part of Kevin's body was injured!!!

Broken bones all over, a four-hour femur surgery, his left leg on the same side—amputated, with them waiting until my daughter Margaret and granddaughter Samantha and I flew in from Virginia and North Carolina to operate on his broken neck!

"Accepting what God allows" was the only way we made it successfully!

Furthermore, to add the ultimate insult to Kevin Sr.'s injury, his oldest 33-year-old son Kevin Jr. in Florida, committed suicide, while Kevin Sr. was sooo hospital-bound!

Well, by this time with me being with so much faith, I still needed Jesus like never before! We all had to muster-up/endure in the biggest "anointed such time/scepter touching" need of our lives, being as a wretch undone! Very soon realizing how we (Kevin Sr.'s family) had to hide our feelings as much as possible, for his emotional welfare and healthful needs! You can just imagine how he felt inside.

I had to let the Lord's sovereignty step-in controlling/consoling my son's very own "anointed such time" need (yes with our help) toward his healing process like never before. Yes, Rocky—his nickname, and was always like the "Rock of Gilbralter." The doctor said, "He's got to prove it now!" You should see how he has proven it so far—three years later. He is in his own house, driving with that good enough right leg thank God! He had been born a 3 ¼ pound premature baby, needing no oxygen! Unto this day, "A skinny little 59-year-old good-looking piece of leather, well put together" man! (smile)

Back to Kevin Jr., we all had just talked to him. I was sure he was on his way to see his father, with no idea of his intention.

Soon afterward the Lord had me to explain to the "family" (where the biggest battleground is) how the enemy is allowed to challenge our awesome oneness of unified powerful families ever—in our choice! And although Kevin Jr. could not avoid him at his weakest stage, we have to let our Lord's anointed power source help us "press-on" through it all! "We each shall be held accountable for our own souls!"

For our children have been taught/trained (Proverb 22:6) the right way to go, often not desiring to totally surrender their all, so The Holy Spirit can lead, guide, and direct them in their "scepter touching of our Lord's anointed such time" needs!!!

To God be all the glory!

Chapter Ten

Saving the Best for Last

I recall seeing Robert "Bob" release his last breath. I knew he heard his last drummer's beat, the last bell being tolled, just as we will too someday. And at the cemetery, I looked down at Robert in his casket. I was so grateful that he received his salvation before leaving this earth on December 11, 2002. I leaned down at Robert's soon-decaying body and spoke to his already-released spirit, his actual saved soul, saying, "Farewell, sweet prince, king, and priest of our home. I'll see you in the morning." Robert's *last* days were truly his *best* days here! Robert knew Christ would never leave him nor forsake him (Hebrews 13:5).

Robert was born in Fayetteville, North Carolina, to the late Sylvester Paul Perara of New Orleans, Louisiana, and the late Lucille W. Perara of Little Rock, Arkansas. He was the father of five children: Keith, Kevin, Mary, Robert Jr, and Margaret. He had two sisters, the late Mary Sue Graham and the late Altae Mae Cliette. Her husband was Lieutenant Colonel Albert Cliette (ret.) of Fayetteville. Robert had two nephews, Eugene Graham (his wife is Carol of Fayetteville) and Michael Cliette (his wife is Tryna of Maryland), and one niece, the late René Cliette. He was also blessed with a host of grandchildren and great-grandchildren.

Robert graduated from E. E. Smith High School in Fayetteville, North Carolina. He was also a young student of the very impressionable Newbold Elementary School (once conveniently located next door to Fayetteville State University). He also attended Wayne Community College, Goldsboro, North Carolina, after his retirement from the US Air Force.

Robert & our Perara children with our Fayetteville Cliette N.C. Family

He was known as Bobby to all, but for the sake of this final chapter, I will call him by his birth name, Robert. He was very serious-minded and dedicated to his church, historical St. Joseph Episcopal in Fayetteville. Robert received a four-year scholarship for St. Augustine Episcopal College in Raleigh, North Carolina. After he truly accepted my call into ministry, he always told me how badly he felt for not being able to take advantage of his scholarship. He asked the Lord to forgive him for failing to obtain his degree. I consoled and shared with him that God had a purpose for his life that needed no explanation. He needed to know that the Lord did not hold it against him, and I truly thanked him for finally accepting and encouraging the furtherance of my educated ministry.

My husband had to make a choice between attending school on his scholarship or joining the air force and having the necessary finances to take care of his mother. He joined the military to take care of his mom. What woman in her right mind would find any problems with that? He joined the air force the very next day after his high school graduation and vowed to take care of his mother. This story regarding Robert's way of thinking always touched my heart. It was a pleasure for her to be getting a monthly allotment also!

It was through the military commitment that he met me[27] on July 2, 1960. He was stationed at Bunker Hill Air Force Base (about thirteen miles from my home) in Kokomo, Indiana. Kokomo is where forty-one years of prosperity began for my family. We began our family journey in the military—with no apologies!

Please allow me to fast-forward for a moment. In 2005, I recall spending my annual Thanksgiving holiday with my family at my daughter Mary's home in Maryland. There I was, in a slightly depressed, melancholy way, reminiscing of Robert. He was with us for Thanksgiving in 2002, which was two weeks before he passed on December 11. His birthday was on November 22; it's sad though, for it's the date our late President John F. Kennedy died. He had always been so blessed with celebrating it mostly on Thanksgiving Day.

Robert turned seventy on November 22, 2002, but he wasn't feeling well that year. He could not eat his favorite Thanksgiving meal, and he was very quiet. Little did we know that his body was in preparation of failing him. He still led us through our family gathering that night. Mary asked each one of us, "What are you most thankful for this year?" He was especially tickled from a response shared by our granddaughter Samantha, who was five years old at the time. She said, "I thank you, Lord, for all of us being together once more. Please help Pappy feel better and the devil be not good to go! Hallelujah!"

The term "good to go" is a military term. In Sammy's five-year-old mind, she was telling the enemy that he was not "good to go" over how her pappy was feeling. Wow, what a comforting prophecy for her to share! None of us were aware of Robert's last two weeks ahead. We were all so amazed of what Samantha said, and he, Robert, gave her such a big hug. It was truly a memorable moment we will never forget! Samantha spoke seed-sowing words. Hallelujah!

---

27 Proverbs 18:22.

Robert always had a heart for children. He was a Wayne County School bus driver for thirteen years, and the kids adored Mr. Bob, as they lovingly called him. They cherished how he used to reward them with soda and candy on report card days. For years, this was something he did from his heart with his own money. Robert always believed in the combination of respect and relationships. His coworkers and children on the bus (and their parents) absolutely thought the world of him! One year he received the Wayne County Bus Driver of the Year award. He truly loved his job and felt that he was making a difference in the lives of the children that rode his bus.

Chief master sergeant Robert h. Perara Sr.honored for his job as Wayne County school; bus driver of year 1994the School Bus children's "Mr. Bob" for 13 yrs.

Let's go back to our 2005 Thanksgiving holiday. It was as if the Lord quickly perked me up, saying, "Don't you shut the door on me, Esther. Don't shut me out. I want to continue using you for my glory" (John 12:23–28). These words inspired me to recall Galatians 6:9, which says, "Let us not grow weary while doing good, for in due season we shall reap if we do not lose heart." The Lord told me to continue to move forward. I pray every morning. "Lord, make me an instrument of your peace and love. Unto Your glory, I count it all joy in the Holy Ghost of God" (James 1:2). I felt that God was pulling on my spirit and it was his desire that I no longer hold the silence of my life.

While I was still in Maryland for Thanksgiving in 2005, the Holy Spirit again encouraged me to begin writing my book. Grandma Joy also gave a confirmation and encouraged me to start writing. Please check out my friend Grandma Joy Whitaker's most wonderful book(s). She is a most inspiring encourager and children's storyteller and destiny image author. I told my daughters that I could not go back home without some clear directions and confirmation regarding the book. I did not know how to begin putting forty years of my life on paper.

My daughter Mary agreed to edit the book once and my daughter Margaret agreed to provide the administrative support. I knew that both of them have very busy schedules, but it was something that I knew they would attempt to do for me. I was still having a hard time following through. Grandma Joy continued to encourage me and gave me the extra push I needed to begin writing. I told my pastor that I might need to go to the mountains someday for seclusion for this writing—that house, like I mentioned in chapter 9, where I was laid up with that meniscus knee also. Well, though I did learn to be careful in what I ask for, I still believed in my sovereign God, still trusting for Him to see me through in all of my "anointed such times!"

I shall never forget Mary's encouraging words that reassured me to think that I could really write my book, my life's story. As I sat on the train on the way home from Mary's house, she called and said, "Mom, just keep putting it all on paper." God has allowed me to keep the best for last. But amazingly, I wrote the notes regarding the last chapter on the train ride home first—having been at my daughter's 2005 Thanksgiving gathering. As God is my witness, I misplaced them somehow but just found them this very hour in 2006! God is an on-time God; yes, He is!

The Lord's hands were truly a blessing to Robert every day, especially in his last days. I now know that Jesus was preparing to receive him. Robert was truly a testimony to all who knew him, and I believe that he received the promised eternal inheritance. His living testimony is present in this book. Although his soul is absent from the body, Robert is very much alive. I obediently share Robert's living testimony with you. Hebrews 9:17 says his testimony is in force now anyhow after his (the testator's) death. Hallelujah!

The last chapter is about Robert, his testimony, and the last days of his predestined life. The Lord spoke to my heart, saying, "Esther, for such a time as this, you remained faithful through your time with your husband, knowing that all things were working together for My sovereign good for you [Romans 8:28]." You believed the good in Robert and his teddy-bear heart as he finally, totally surrendered to Me before his last year on this earth.

I was always encouraged of God's promises over my life. The Lord reminded me of His yeahs and amens as they reign true even among doubters, which is the favorite verse (2 Corinthians 1:20) of one of my local spiritual son-pastors, Rev. Ivan T. Davis, who's always sowing into my life for me to be encouraged. I thank God for all that He has done in my life. There were other words of encouragement that the Lord offered to me regarding Robert's life. Some were my thoughts, but the time I spent with the Lord regarding Robert made me think of the following:

1. "Esther, remember how your pastor, Bishop Smith, reminds you of your favorite quote, 'A blessing delayed is not a blessing denied.'"
2. I remind you of a comment your pastor said, "Brother Bob made it in, I do believe, before it was everlastingly too late for him!" I have to say, with the signs and wonders that followed, I know that he did. I know that I received the answer to a lifetime of prayers.
3. Once Robert was saved, he released the will of the Lord in his life. He was saved, born again, and truly set free unto eternal everlasting peace.

4. Robert learned what standing on the promises of God meant, and he put everything in the master's hand.
5. Robert also learned as he watched me (Esther) walk my Christian life with God through Jesus Christ. My life exemplified the mentality of "If I perish, I perish."[28] With this mentality, Robert said, "Point well taken."
6. "Robert saw you (Esther) sell out to Me. You showed him the way, truth, and life" (John 14:6).
7. Robert denied himself, took up his passionate cross daily, and followed the Lord.

While Robert was on the dialysis machine, it gave him time to think about his life. I know Jesus was throwing out a lifeline for him to catch. I often wondered what his thoughts were on a daily basis in the last days of his life. I chose to believe that Robert walked into his purpose and his salvation as I saw Christ working in him.

I remember a message I gave in Durham, North Carolina, a few years back during the hurricane season. The topic was "There Is Power in the Water,"[29] and the subtopic was "It's an Inside Job." It was to remind that the living waters of Christ Jesus (Word of God) is designed to root out, cleanse, and purge us inwardly. Robert's dialysis machine might have drained his physical strength, but his spiritual living soul was saturated and filled with the very best of Christ forevermore.

I had never known Robert without bow legs. On our first wedding day, he happily walked me out, slinging those legs down the aisle of Bunker Hill AFB Chapel, Indiana, near my home in Kokomo on August 4, 1961 (the same day President Barack Obama was being born in Hawaii). By the way, lovely Michelle and I have the same birthdates—January 17—and we have another connection. On their October 3 anniversary, my Keith and Mary (four years apart) celebrate their birthdays!

---

[28] Esther 4:16.

[29] John 7:38.

Robert was on crutches for many years before his passing. His infirmity never stopped him from witnessing to those in need. He was never complaining! You were subject to see him anywhere, especially after he was saved! He was not ashamed of the gospel of Jesus Christ, for it is the power of God unto salvation for everyone who believes.[30]

In Robert's last days, he was testifying and praising God, rejoicing for his many blessings. Although his surgery for his knees was prolonged by forty to fifty years, he finally agreed to have the surgery one leg at a time (within the same year that he passed away). He was certainly determined to serve the Lord in that year—his *last* but *best* forevermore!

Robert always desired to leave this earth the way he came in—with both legs straight. In his casket, he was able to lie in as such. We had his casket fully opened, which showed that his legs were very straight while he wore his military uniform. He used to say that he just did not feel right in any clothing other than his military uniform. Even though his body in his earthly walk was no longer with us, he certainly looked his best in his uniform on the day of his home-going service. He would have been very pleased!

Chapter 4 spoke about "going for broke," which means "to give it all to Christ" (1 Peter 5:6). Robert humbled himself under the mighty hand of God in every phase of total submission. More importantly, he asked for forgiveness and forgave everyone that he needed to reconnect with. Robert was at peace when he left this earth, and I believe this was the most significant reason. He was very serious about the Father's business, and he wanted to leave a spiritual legacy of the love of Christ to the present and future generations of the Perara family and to everyone else he was connected with.

In the Bible, 1 Corinthians 7:14 says, "For the unbelieving husband is sanctified by the wife, and the unbelieving wife is sanctified by the husband; otherwise your children would be unclean, but now they are Holy."[31] I could probably write a book on this scripture

---

[30] Romans 1:16.

[31] 1 Corinthians 7:14.

alone. Ephesians 5:21–33 provides us with spiritual instructions for the husbands and wives regarding marriages.[32] A marriage does not make it over forty years without its trials. I thank the Lord for teaching me what true perseverance means. It gave me the strength to see my husband receive his salvation two years before he passed in May 2000. Our home was complete when Robert made the ultimate decision.

I remember the women in my life (my mama, grandmothers, aunties, etc.) that prayed over the men in my family. They also prayed for my life and my sister, Laney, too for our purpose and destiny. Isaiah 59:19 says, "When the enemy comes in like a flood, the Spirit of the Lord will lift up a standard against him." Haman's evil spirit is very active today as he is trying to destroy the very relationships of the men in our lives. Women of God, let's encourage one another to pray without ceasing for the holy, reverent fear of God to return to the priests and kings of our homes. Our children and grandchildren are watching us, and we need to show them the power of God through our prayers. If we could let His power show us how to be on record with our believed-for prayers, we would be a phenomenal nation, lacking nothing.

The Perara family's Thanksgiving gathering at Mary's was the primary birthing location of the predestined physical account for my book. On the train heading home in November 2005, I cannot tell you how strange it felt to feverishly begin writing my book. Interestingly, I wrote the last chapter first. Thereafter, every morning, I would have revelations and more revelations for my book. However, I was so blessed to see the final chapter helping me to begin writing the rest of the book. Isn't it like God to remind us that our ways are not His ways?

It is always in my heart to be my family's Biblical Esther spirit because my truest desire is to see all my family members saved. The Lord knows that I cast my cares on Him for He cares for me.[33] God cares for everyone in my family and every soul I touch to not only be

---

[32] Ephesians 5:21–33.

[33] 1 Peter 5:7.

saved but to prosper and to have a true relationship with Him. We must not just talk about it, but we have to walk it in our daily lives.

The initial title to this chapter was "Do Not Forget Mordecai." The theme was "making a difference by encouraging someone." The day I met my husband, I felt that God was sending me the heart of Mordecai all over again. Uncle Bill was my first Mordecai and encouraged me during my teenage and young adult years. My husband, Robert, cared very deeply for me and supported me during my married years. God was showing me that Uncle Bill officially passed the spiritual baton to Robert, my second Mordecai. Also, as I reflect back, Robert's father passed away when Robert was twelve years old, and my hardworking father and Uncle Bill's powerful life of Christ living was an influence in Robert's life. It's dormant and proven mentorship!

Uncle Bill would not have trusted Robert so easily if he did not have a great relationship with him. Robert really got along with my grandmothers also. They always loved and respected his old-fashioned mannerism and character. In many ways, he was very much like my old-fashioned father and reminded me of the stature my father and Uncle Bill carried as a person.

Bishop Smith shared that the word *lord* in the Bible means "responsible king" and "priest authority of the home." In the Bible, 1 Peter 3:6 says, "Sarah obeyed Abraham calling him the little lord." Sarah knew Abraham was God's will and way for their home. Although I never called Robert lord, I knew that it was God's will for us to love, respect, and honor each other, submitting to each other as unto the Lord (Ephesians 5:22–23). That which was always lacking I just left it to the Lord's anointed presence for my going through "such times!" However, we knew in our hearts we were meant to be. Reflect back on our chosen similarities in chapter 3.

My sisters and brothers, some of the most awesome and revealing things catapulted my mind and truly touched my heart. I saw my second Mordecai in Robert as God went to work in him through mothering sometimes. In his last days, Robert had allowed himself to release things in his life to let the Lord control (including some areas in our marriage). He truly allowed me to see the best of Robert in his last days. He supported the ministry that I was committed to and even asked me to pray for him many times on our knees. Yes, Robert, the spiritual leader of our household, would lead in prayer too!

I was blessed to be able to preside at our 11:00 a.m. church service on his last Sunday here as he passed away two days later. At home that night, his comments were touching with more *constructive* criticism! Robert. My second Mordecai began helping me by sharing his remarks. As I previously mentioned, he would say, "Esther, when you get your church, I'm going to be your assistant pastor." We would laugh about that quite a bit. Oh, how we had come such a long way in order for him to make that comment! It truly spoke volumes of the level of support he offered before his life ended. God is great, and He is so faithful! Great is Thy faithfulness, Lord God!

As I reflected back to the two weeks after our annual Thanksgiving gathering, I was reminded how a person feels better just before they leave this earth. It is as if God is allowing our last time on earth to be our *best* scepter-touching anointed times! Of course, we know there is nothing better than being with Him when our purpose has been fulfilled. God desires for us to live out our last and best days in Him. God watches over us even in the end. The most glorious song sung at Robert's home-going was "God Is." He is the joy and the strength of our lives, and He is our all in all and everything we want Him to be! This song was released over Robert's home-going because it reminded me that God is everything we need Him to be—our strength, provider, healer, shelter, comforter, etc. I thank the Lord for His versatility to be what we need at any moment in our lives—with our God's spiritual-scepter touching and spiritual Esther's anointed "such times."

The day before Robert's passing, (before I went to work) I prayed over him. I reminded him that everyone was so proud of him as he fought his ailments. He patiently accepted being hooked to his dialysis system all night at home until later in the morning the next day. He would have to stay home until later in the day while his family came and went as needed. Bob chose those quiet times to cover his family in prayer. We heard later that he had witnessed to quite a few people later that day. Hallelujah!

Saints, the day before he passed, I saw many areas of my life were being fulfilled. I thought of where my life was before I met him, and I thought of our wonderful marriage. I also reminisced of our family life together and our dedication to live a good life, better able to accept the bad with the good life! I realized at that moment the Lord was preparing me for ministry. Robert knew his last days were going to pull the best out of me and eventually him. He certainly had years of ministry of endurance and perseverance.

I still feel Robert's continuous prayers, and I know that they are still covering me to this very day. I feel his prayers each time I go forth, committed to the great commission of Christ. God has given us His powerful anointing, and we can rely on the fulfillment of His mission for us. God has chosen us to share His anointing and His Word. He could have chosen anything He desired to share His anointing with, but He chose us.

Robert knew I lived by the age-old song "Lift Him Up" and that, though I had to just live a forty-year life of satisfied praises to the Lord, he eventually found out I was simply seeking the Lord's kingdom first and His righteousness (Matthew 6:33–34)! It was true worshipful lifestyle through it all! This is what the enemy fights against—"just Jesus" in us, not us, knowing we already have been conquered by Him (Isaiah 53:1–5). I just kept trusting but in stubborn faith and believing His promises, especially how, by His way at His will, he would add all other things unto me (and my family)! Yes, Lord, You in Your own sovereign-anointed scepter-touching needs for us Esther spirits are trusted for your drawing all men unto you (John 12:32)! I wait, worshipping God in spirit and in truth (John 4:24), for my heart is to live a true lifestyle of a worshipper as an anointed server toward His needy people!

Biblical studies Bachelor Science (B.S.)Graduation day w/ bishop Chester L. Aycock & vice bishop Richard w. Johnson

When I did receive the blessing to pursue my official ministry from my husband, it was a very exciting moment that seemed to fall in place in our home and in our lives. We should be more encouraging as each of us fulfills our unselfish prospective ministry. There is truly a need to lift the name of Jesus on a daily basis. John 13:34–35 gives us a commandment to love one another as Christ loves us. We need to truly be disciples of Christ and to have unconditional love for one another, yes, but let's not miss the *last and best* line of John 13:34, 35, which is on love of Christ from one to another! We can say we love one another all day long, but the grace and mercy of Jesus Christ is patiently waiting (till He says it's over) for us to put His unconditional love into action! We can do it if we just allow the Holy Spirit to help us.

In the spiritual charge on our lives, we should possess a go-getter attitude. Let's pray for one another to fulfill the work of our ministry. It is God's will that the promises and commandment to love manifest in us. We believe in the report of the Lord and His promises of yea and amen.[34] I am sold out to believe *we can be* a church without spots nor wrinkles that Christ will come back for,[35] and the Lord's Word is all the proof I need.

The Lord said *we* shall do even greater works,[36] and in my heart (it's a mind-set), I continue believing in the "we"! There are those that will have a criticizing spirit and may not agree with anything that is done for the glory of God. The important thing for us to do is to walk by faith and not by sight. We must believe in our walk with God, knowing that He is pleased at our efforts. I choose to keep God's commandments and abide by His love so that I may have an abundant life,[37] unselfishly praying for the family of God.

My Robert learned before he passed that it was all right to sell out our lives to Christ. I am so thankful that Jesus rose after the crucifixion and burial for us. His light should shine everywhere we go in our worshipful lifestyle. Christ is the true vine, and we are His branches. Let's network into His system so we can produce good fruit.[38]

Pastors and spiritual leaders should not be intimidated of our remote, distant services for the Lord even. Is it not for His Holy Ghost's spiritual design to lead, guide, and direct the many of us in each mission toward the Acts 2:47 souls that should be you reaching one when I can't? We should be an army of one—this true church of the Living God. Matthew 18:20 says, "For where two or three are gathered together in My name [even in His Spirit in us], I am there in the midst of them." We all at St. Mark Church were so grateful for our pastor's God-given vision of the November family month.

---

[34] Isaiah 53:1–5.

[35] Ephesians 5:27.

[36] John 14:12.

[37] John 10:10; 15:10.

[38] John 15:1.

Esther along w/ Jordan Hamilton attempting my Indiana basketball (smile) days at St. Mark's November Family Month Park outing

In the park, my Indiana basketball days came out in me a little bit. While witnessing to others, Jesus is always in the midst of us when we serve Him. God is calling us to come out of the four walls of the church and minister to those that are really in need. I thank God for my pastor, General Bishop Alton Smith; our spiritual mother, Lady Doris Smith; and our church, St. Mark's Church of Christ, disciples of Christ. It is so good to see everyone consistently giving their heart to the ministry. They have a true desire to see people everywhere in fellowship with one another—like Lady D's (as she has us call her) blessed Women of the Mark (WOTM) monthly shared gathering and most exhilarating yearly South Carolina beach retreats. Spiritual sisters get to know one another better but, most of all, have fellowship with one another unto relationships!

At one of our weekly prayer services, my pastor asked each of the attendees to share one sentence of the Sinner's Prayer. The request was truly an amazing experience and promoted unity among us. There were other ways of fellowship that we were involved in to include the Emmaus Walk under the leadership of Bishop Valerie Melvin for our local assembly of the singles' ministry. It was very clear that the commemorative Emmaus Walk was very much needed.

Dr. William Barber II—president of the North Carolina chapter of the NAACP, the local stop the Funeral Initiative Inc. for years against youth violence, drugs, and gangs, etc., and pastor of Greenleaf Christian Church, Goldsboro—also set the precedence of our inspirational morning by eloquently speaking on the very purpose of our walk with "Knowing the Purpose of God for Our Lives." As a man of God serving faithfully in the community, he enlightened us by expounding in the areas of the following:

1. Sharing Jesus together ("Let's walk, and let's talk about it")
2. Transforming the Word of God in prayer
3. Letting the Holy Spirit lead, adjust, and shape the agendas

Everyone that attended these events truly felt the presence of God and His love to see His children fellowship together. When two or more people are committed to make a connection, God is always going to strengthen the relationship for His glory! It is my prayer that we love one another and let God abide in us, for His love has been perfected in *us*. We are to release Christ in us and recognize that He who is in us is greater than he who is in the world.[39]

The Emmaus Walk was a designated time after the Resurrection of Jesus and was a lifesaver for the disciples. We see an example of two people walking and talking to each other to help each other see the light and be set free. They are speaking to Jesus, and they do not realize that it is Him initially (Luke 24:14–15). In verse 16, we see Jesus drawing near them in their obedience as they walk, talk, and reason together. They were true instruments of fellowship, and Jesus was in the midst of them. He shared scripture and abided with the two men. Then Jesus had communion with them, and their eyes opened. They immediately recognized who Christ was, and He departed from them. He left them, saying, "Do we recognize with our spiritual eyes opened our one spiritual heart burn within us for Christ?"

39 1 John 4:4.

The story of Jesus appearing on the road to Emmaus with the two men is a classic example of fellowship. Christ was and will always be in the people business. He could not pass up the opportunity to show His love for these two people. They were truly honored by His presence and couldn't contain themselves with what they saw. We are to lead others into an acquaintance and fellowship with Christ and with others to lift Him up and to draw unto Him.[40] We must also allow the scriptures to penetrate our minds, open our eyes, inspire us to share, and spread the knowledge of Christ. I want to demonstrate God's unconditional love to His people, which truly pleases Him.

God's anointing is in the midst of us, especially the saints, who are working together in His name and believing in Him for answered prayers. Christ desires for us to live, share, and give of ourselves to His kingdom. I was asked to come join in a panel-speaking engagement at a Washington, DC, Annual Ecumenical Conference. *Ecumenical* means "from the whole world" (Romans 8:22). It was a conference concerning the Christian Church as a whole. The purpose of the conference was to further the unification of Christian Church movements to promote cooperation and a better understanding among the various religious faiths. I had been ready for it, but it was cancelled. The Lord makes no mistakes, for the planned agenda has permeated within me forever. It gave me a purposed oneness-minded journey like never before, which also was another good influence in this writing, confirming Robert's blessed military career (oneness seen later in this chapter).

The Word says, "Jesus came, He Saw and He Conquered [Romans 8:37] for us all." Acts 17:26 says, "And He has from One blood every nation of men to dwell on all the face of the earth." One of my Pastor General Bishop Alton A. Smith's very favorite. The desire of Christ is for all of us to become one in Him from out of our denominations, races, mentalities, or creed. He also desires for us to accept the spirit of unity and accept Him as Lord and Savior. The theme of the conference was to be "One Lord, One Faith and One Baptism." As children of Christ, we are to live in a world with

---

[40] Luke 24:31; John 12:32.

different diversities of gifts but of the same Spirit of Christ[41] so God's people can be an example for others. The Holy Spirit will also teach us to live together, work together, and worship with one another as we strive to be on one accord.

I only pray that these conferences will go on to be a lifetime remembrance to us all wherever we are. Conferring in the amazing, graceful, anointed Esther spirit of our Lord's great commission unto His scepter-touching oneness purpose!

I just want to live my life in Christ and for it not to be lived in vain.[42] Equally, I do not want God's living Word within me to return void. It is Christ's desire that our souls prosper.[43] As we submit to His will, we must trust in His grace and believe Him for the rest as He gives us His very best.

I've spoken about the military in this book because it was Robert's diligent and devoted career. Most of the children's lives (and my adult life) were invested into the military. Military life was a very beneficial, committing, and challenging lifestyle. We took it very seriously, but we created a lifetime of enjoyment and incredible memories everywhere we went.

Military families encourage and support one another through the good times and the difficult times. Although each one of us is accountable for our own souls, we need to continue to encourage one another to reach our Salvation in Christ before it is too late. I believe that we are entering into that moment in time where it is getting late in the evening of time and the *sun* is beginning to go down on some lives. Don't we want to latch on to the *Son* of the Living God? The passion of our souls to be saved for the kingdom of God is for everyone we touch along the way. It truly does not matter whether you are in the military, a civilian spouse of a military soldier, or a civilian that is not affiliated with the military. It is my family's desire to see everyone receive their salvation in Christ. In this chapter, let's focus on the military family.

---

41 I Corinthians 12:4–12.

42 3 John 2.

43 Psalms 133:1.

The Bible says, "Behold, how good and pleasant it is for brethren to dwell together in unity!"[44] The military has a unique code of unity. We are trained and equipped to accomplish a mission and to accomplish the mission *together*! It is more important to activate the buddy system (looking out for one another) than being concerned about a person's race or where they were raised. When duty calls, we perform it *together*.

Robert and I had a lifelong marriage and a wonderful family. We love and adore our five beautiful children. Each child participated in so many activities. At any given time, we were going to basketball games, baseball games, football games, cheerleading, swimming lessons, bowling, etc. We needed a daily meeting just to keep up with the activities of each child! We truly loved the military life. Robert was chosen to be the president of the bowling leagues every season. Of course, I supported his position, which kept us pretty busy most nights of the week—not to mention how Robert's chief master sergeant status and superintendent of squadrons landed him in many prestigious nighttime outings. Yes, of course, being my committed self, I went along too.

The children also had school affairs consisting of birthday parties, outdoor and indoor movie theater participations in Guam, beautiful family park functions, and frequent beach outings. Almost everyone on the military base would be invited to the Guamanian luau parties, where they celebrated family birthdays, weddings, and anniversaries. Governor Camacho's always teased me about the day he kissed my hand; I wondered if I would ever wash my hand again. Well, the fair anointed favor of God was at work on this Esther spirit! Robert and I decided that if the children were going to have fun, then we were also.

Every month, we would invite families to the monthly affairs of the noncommissioned officers' (NCO) wives' club. The NCO's club wives performed various projects to include community work at several nursing homes, group home involvements, and charitable

---

[44] Isaiah 55:11.

events. I was blessed to receive the outstanding Young Women of America Award at K. I. Sawyer Air Force Base (AFB) in Michigan.

Although I truly appreciated the award, it is the work performed there that I will cherish most. I've looked at the book one time. I enjoyed my duties as a military wife and mother with its special "such times" provisions from our awesome God's anointed scepter-touching needs! Actually, it was further instrumental toward this Esther spirit's determined family oneness!

The moments that I am sharing with you is freeing me even more as I write. Hallelujah! The children and I (and other military families) went to various sporting events and watched our husbands and fathers play ball, umpire, or referee. Robert even formed a youth basketball league of all ages. Yes, our children and I supported it big time! We even took time to ride all the way to the United States naval facilities on the island for entertainment and mega shopping. They did not want to leave the Guam, sure enough! That amusement park being under construction might have been the straw that broke the camel's back for this ole girl!

We also attended the base chapel's church services. The children were young and very impatient if the service was longer than an hour. Robert knew that we needed to be in church, but he could only last for about an hour himself during this time in his life. All I could do was be grateful that we were attending church together as a family. I believe there are other military wives that understand and share my experience. We are all in this together! I knew there was much more that God was going to do in His master plan for our lives. This Esther spirit just knew, above all things, to seek Him first for such tremendous anointing power for the scepter-touching needed!

Our family traveled extensively. As a military family, you become very accustomed to traveling. Every two to three years, Robert would receive military orders to another military installation that would require for us to relocate. We wondered about the impact on how the relocations would affect the children. One year, the children were enrolled in three different schools for the highly unusual three moves within one year. Socially, they would have to make new friends, only to leave them again and again to relocate and make new friends. On a positive note, the relocations allowed them to enhance their communication skills, which kept them socially grounded. I don't think any of our children are hesitant to strike up a conversation with almost anyone.

The military is about people, and we knew it was second to the church body as a people business. The military taught our children about responsibility, education, culture, and social characteristics. Robert had a motto he used to have us join in all the time. He would say, "Ain't this living!" All of us shouted, "Yeah!" We do thank the Lord for giving us a chance to know what *real true living* in Jesus Christ is all about!

Throughout the years of military living, there were various activities that we played for monetary winnings. The grown folks would send the children outside to play, and we would clear the dining room table to play cards. I personally put the *p* in *pinochle*, the *t* in *tonk*, the *w* in *whist*, and the *s* in *spades*, etc.! Yes, me! Another game that was played a lot was bingo. It wasn't until decades later that I realized we should not have been playing for money. Now I understand for some families and households, monetary games are okay (to each his own).

I am certainly not trying to be judgmental; however, for our household in the present time, we recognize it as a form of gambling and choose not to participate in card games for money. I realize that Mark 8:36 says, "For what will it profit a man if he gains the whole world, and lose his own soul?" Some of you know it could truly become very appealing. There were alternate games we decided to play with the children. These games included Trouble, slapjack, "I declare war" (with cards), concentration, Pictionary, and of course, Monopoly among the traditional board games. These games were awesome to play on weekends and during snow days and power outages. We had fifty foot snowdrifts at K. I. Sawyer AFB, Marquette, Michigan, the entire winter!

The Bible says, "My God shall supply all of our needs according to His riches in glory in Christ Jesus" (Philippians 4:19). For our children, we later learned the importance of teaching them to wait on the Lord regarding their provisional needs. They needed to learn the difference between luck and blessings. They needed to learn that you can live without luck but you can't live on this earth without the blessings of the Lord.

Robert and I believed in providing our children with a good life and a well-rounded atmosphere. There were times that God was making the decisions for us. I stayed home with our children until our youngest daughter, Margaret, was able to attend kindergarten. I was branch manager for RCA Global Communication at the Anderson AFB Terminal in Guam for two years. There were many times (as a military dependent) when Robert believed that I was unable to do certain things on my own. He was so shocked when I told him he never let me! Plus, I was so conveniently happy to see my family (especially him and his heavily committed military service) prevail successfully!

Truly an Esther's anointed "Such Time" at the most horrendous job-ever heard-of!
Branch mgr at the RCA Global Communication - Anderson AFB Agana Guam Terminal! 1972-1974

The RCA position was one of the most horrendous jobs I ever had or ever heard of. I worked for the company during the most dangerous Vietnam War operations of the 1970s. The main RCA office only wanted one employee at a time to work at this particular site, but I was able to have support the last four hours of each day. As the war continued, the airmen would make their transitions on the base and then fly back and forth to the war zone via the Guam AFB terminal.

The best way to describe a particular day on my *fast-paced* job at RCA is as follows: Lines of soldiers were formed from one end of the terminal to the other to make phone calls to their loved ones at home. Sometimes these calls were "Dear, John" phone calls, where wives or girlfriends would leave the relationship of their loved one right over the phone. Of course, some of these airmen would end up banging, kicking, kicking, and even tearing down booths! Next there were telegrams to be sent, mostly the overnight, immediate, and fastest way. This particular task in itself kept me on my feet. And even though the troops saw my detailed information for telegram instructions posted nearby, they would still inquire about telegram procedures—while many things were happening at once! They would always be asking if their telegrams made it home yet, and being the only form of such communication available to make before they went to war, they had to know that the delivery went through. Besides the different types of telegrams, each one had to be processed immediately on my Telex machine, *going straight through*! The telephone would be ringing nonstop, even with inquiries about any returned telegram responses.

Mind you, whenever the main RCA office in Aghana Guam would call, or ping for my attention on my Telex, I had to answer immediately! Also, there was the changing of the Telex machine tape—all at the same time period! Oh yes, do not forget the conducting of the three telephone booths at the same time!

By the way, when I made my bank run every morning, I had to experience them watching me like a hawk for my expediency! However, they did have to put up with me and wait for me to report on the Telex before going and returning. My, my, my, were they waiting for me and the incoming and the incoming telegrams also!

The farthest one I had to send (in return) was Hong Kong! Can you imagine all these events happening simultaneously at nearly the same time?

Yes, truly this Esther's ultimate challenge for God's spiritual-scepter touching. Surely my "anointed such times" were needed!

My dear sisters and brothers, I continue to thank God that I can be used for His glory! I am no better than our John 12:23–28. Jesus Christ made the true ultimate sacrifice for each of us. God says He's ready to do it again and again for us! One thing's for sure, *this* humble child of God could not have gone through any stormy trials of life without His anointed presence that will never leave nor forsake us (Hebrews 13:5b).

We see more and more how much praying we're to do for one another when we come into each other's mind. I truly asked the Lord, "Do I have to touch another typewriter?" Well, I do thank Him for being able to buy Robert a new 1975 Cadillac when we returned back to the States! *I did* my family sacrifice!

Moreover, these military troops need to constantly be encouraged and prayed for. Please pray for their souls to find the true peace of God and calmness in the midst of all their stormy trials and their families.

I truly felt (with 1 John 3:17) compassion for these troops; I did not even know what kind of mental state I would be in if I knew I was about to go into such a war zone! Selah, think on it! Furthermore, just think of the threefold care most of them need upon their return back home (physical, spiritual, emotional, etc.). I do believe there is more posttraumatic stress disorder (PTSD) among them these recent war days more than ever before—even undetected!

On a brighter note, I was especially grateful for the very special on-time USO entertainment afforded these devoted beautiful men and women warriors. Bob Hope would come through that terminal to honor the troops heading for war. He would bring Lola Falana, Loni Anderson, Tina Turner, the Dallas Cowboy Cheerleaders, and more to raise the morale of the troops; this always seemed to work. All I could do was throw my hands up, shouting "Hallelujah," and to keep on working! Helen Baylor's song says, "If it had not been for the Lord on my side, tell me, where would I be?"

To our Christian soldiers, great is your task to not only fight for your country in wartime but also finding the time to save the souls of your fellow soldiers. Our prayers extend to you because you already understand the importance of salvation, particularly on the front lines of a very active war that can strike anywhere in the world at any time. Your church families thank you for taking your spiritual stance very seriously.

To the soldiers who have not decided upon salvation for your souls, I pray that the Lord speaks to your heart and that you open your mind and invite Him in so you can hear from God directly or through the chaplains or another soldier who already has a relationship with Christ. The body of Christ is truly praying for your salvation. Your lives are valuable, and your mission is enormous. Your family, friends, loved ones, and nation do not take what you do for granted. We understand that your sacrifice comes with a price, and we do pray for more and more of you to come to believe and pray for that price to be eternal in your life. Please know that you are greatly appreciated for your service to our country, and our prayers for you will *never* cease.

Romans 10:9–10 says, "That if you confess with your mouth the Lord Jesus, and believe in your heart that God has raised Him from the dead, you will be saved. For, with the heart one believes unto righteousness, and with the mouth confession is made unto salvation." As Christians, we must do all we can to encourage our troops, lift them up to Christ, support them, and pray they will accept Him.

People of God, as I pour out my heart to you, I am constantly thinking of the husbands, wives, sons, daughters, parents, etc., that did not survive all the wars we have recently fought and the previous wars that are now a part of our history forever. We must not hesitate any longer to meet people where they are and help them see the significance of their salvation in Christ. Lord, it is my prayer that I am able to help in the saving of many souls and that you will allow me to be that instrument in Your scepter touching in their many needs!" May their Esther spirit anointed times truly empower, encourage, and lead them especially in the last days. For some like my Robert, it would be their very best days ahead!"

In 1974, we returned to Robert's last military assignment to Seymour Johnson AFB in North Carolina. His family is from Fayetteville, which is approximately sixty-five miles from Goldsboro. Our entire family was happy and content to live somewhere for a long period of time. We were so used to moving boxes and going to new military assignments. My children marveled at the fact that they would make new friends that they could actually grow up with!

From 1985 to 1988, I experienced tremendous pain throughout my body that was unbearable. If I was ever going to be in a high level of pain that would have such an impact on me for three years, I am so glad the Lord blessed me with Robert's help! He proved (especially in those moments) that he took our marriage vows very seriously. My body was tortured with excruciating pain twenty-four hours a day, seven days a week. Robert must have thought that I would not be in this world too much longer. But God! Thank God for His Esther spirit "such time" anointing for us!

None of the doctors knew what was wrong with my back. I met with several civilian doctors, but they were unable to pinpoint the problem. I also went to the base hospital, where they decided to air-evacuate me to Portsmouth, Virginia, for one month and then to Walter Reid Army Medical Center, Washington, DC, twice. The last time I was at Walter Reid, I was there for three months. I was truly trying to find out what was wrong. Although I continued to have faith to deal with it, the pain was extremely severe. There was a considerable amount of pinching and throbbing pain shooting all the way around my left side, and I did not know where it was coming from. For three years, I could not sit at all. I had to lay on my right side all night. I couldn't even stand for my clothing to touch those areas. This pain was sheer torture!

While at Walter Reid, none of the medicine was working, and I had tried them all. I had every x-ray and every test you could name. The total tests valued at one million dollars! At some point, I felt that the doctors did not believe I was in extensive pain. When I spoke with them regarding my back, I told them each time exactly where the pain was located. It was in the same area. I felt the same way every single time their specialist came two and three times a day. It was even more frustrating for me that they hesitated to believe me. I even consulted with the pain clinic doctor and especially the surgeon, urging him to operate! Though I was ever so amazingly agile/mobile, walking even to the hospital commander's office, it could very well be the reason for all their apprehension and doubt of my pain! I had initially wanted to avoid the surgical route at all cost, but the pain was just unbearable at this point. I stood my ground on what I knew to be true regarding the pain in my back and side. They would have easily experimented and heeded to my final demands, but God, they refused!

Multiple (six) MRIs were provided, and it was finally revealed that there was a slight curvature (I never knew I had) that was pressing on my spine nerve. The curvature was creating a tremendous pinch and a throbbing pain. God knew, and I knew the test I had to walk through during this season of my life. There were specialists from six DC and Maryland major hospitals, who sat at a round-table discussion to review all my records and x-rays. They strongly stated that I would end up paralyzed for the severity of my situation. I politely and gratefully thanked them and said, "Man's extremity is God's opportunity." After they air-evacuated me back to North Carolina, I put myself on calcium, which I still continue. After three years, it all lifted miraculously!

I decided to share this story because it was a horrible time in my life and Robert was willing to walk through the entire ordeal with me. My best days with my husband included this moment in my life. The doctors took an extensive amount of time to diagnose my pain; Robert cared for me like I were a baby. Robert held me over the commode for those three dedicated faithful years! Man (woman), that's love! He took me to church with all my pillows so I could lay on the pews and receive the sermon messages. I laid on my side for three solid years and never had bed sores. He truly loved and supported me. I will never forget those days in my life. My faith in the Lord healed my spirit, my mind, my soul, and my body.

Under Robert's tough, macho image, he had the heart of a teddy bear and a compassionate spirit. I chose to believe God was going to heal me and remove the pain my body was experiencing. The last day being spent at the hospital was truly my *best day*. With Robert's encouragement and with the hand of God's Holy Spirit stirring/helping me to be finally healed of all the pain that tried to grip me and steal my joy, I feel I passed a three-year major test in my body and another test of perseverance in my marriage!

Praise be to God for these days also and forevermore. My trusting in Him still remains true through it all. At this writing, it's about twenty-five years since that (1985-1988) pain. And can you believe that two months ago 2010, it has just now returned, though more intense than the first days?

The major hospital in our area, the wonderful Pitt County Memorial Hospital, Greenville, North Carolina, found out from one MRI that I have a *degenerated disc* that just didn't show up yet twenty-five years ago. However, they are very normal these days even though the pain reoccurring even baffles the doctors.

Once I got over the shock of it all, I was quickly reminded about who was in control of my life! God, through His Holy Spirit of Jesus Christ in me, went to work as He only knows how. All that kept coming back to me was my pastor, Bishop Smith's, favorite saying, "Whatever He [God] takes you to, He can take you through it!" It left me in my Esther spirit of Christ's anointing in me in such a "touching the spiritual scepter of God" time as never before in my life!

After the severe, excruciating pain left me, it hindered my entire muscle mobility. This time, I took no more all-familiar narcotics. We found that muscle relaxant does work, especially when I went home after being I denied a back surgery; I knew it would be my responsibility afterward. No, I've had no more of my Robert's TLC (tender loving care). It was just Jesus alone sure enough now!

The children did what they could, and Margaret and Mary were outstanding until I had to release them to their home affairs. My church (St. Mark) has certainly shown themselves strong in the Lord's love and compassion (1 John 3:17). I released home health and physical therapy and even gave up chiropractic therapy. They tell us also to eat a lot of Jell-O or gelatin.

Guess what? Whatever triggered this 2010 drama for me, the Lord reminded me of how He had allowed this honey and cinnamon I've faithfully taken four years straight to heal that meniscus knee (both knees really). Well, after all this, others have been somewhat a temporary fix. I feel better and better (though gradually) with this honey and cinnamon. I believed total manifestation in this degenerated-spine healing also! Speaking positive to all about it, I said, "In *everything*, I give thanks" (1 Thessalonians 5:18). I do believe without a shadow of a doubt that I would've been worse today or sooner without the biblical Genesis 43:11 and Exodus 30:22, 23 herb and spice. Also, they are purging purifiers, for I drink at least a glass of water with it each time.

I am not telling anyone what to do; I'm just blessed to be able to give a living testimony and blessing to others of how I got over my ailment!

Bishop Chester L. Aycock of our Goldsboro Raleigh District Assembly, International Inc., Goldsboro, North Carolina, in October 2006, an EMT (emergency Medical Technician) suggested to us that the honey and cinnamon could heal anything in your body. Well, my knee was hurting bad enough that I immediately started on it! I do not know who else had done so, but I had to be extremely faithful about it over these four years. I was sure to drink enough water with the dosage in my same morning tooth-brushing routine and at bedtime. I use the immune system instructions, giving me a "clean bill of health" in the doctor's visits most of the time. The one thing I urge others to do is to continue your doctor's visits, especially before the first dosage! Doctors and nurses have copies even. I keep them for others with me always just in case. But if anyone is interested, "The Power Hour" website is www.thepowerhour.com/news/honey.htm. Be blessed. To God be all the glory!

As I wrap up this chapter, I must share a major event that happened to Robert in 1993. I had just given up my bingo addiction two weeks before. Hallelujah! On January 3, 1993, Robert experienced shortness of breath. Our daughter Margaret drove her father and me (over ninety miles an hour) to the base hospital at Seymour Johnson AFB, Goldsboro, which was five minutes away. It was the last night they received patients at the base emergency room on weekends. If we had to go all the way to Wayne Memorial Hospital (our county hospital) in the city that night (in order for Robert to be treated), (the doctors said) he would not have made it. Isn't that like God? Hallelujah!

Immediately as they put him on the table to cut his clothes, the monitor flat-lined. The code-blue staff and equipment were flying down the hall. God favored me by allowing the staff to keep the doors opened so I would be able to see all the things that was happening to Robert. I looked at his eyes, and they were fixed. His mouth was open, and he was gray in color. The Lord spoke to me and said, "Stretch your hands out, and I'll tell you what to say." Satan wants us to be weak, but I didn't have time for him nor for tears. My daughter Margaret probably thought that I was out of my mind, especially without expressing any tears. The enemy wants you weak in these vulnerable moments! I told Margaret to go park her car since her motor was still running.

I stretched out my hands and said, "Satan, get your hands off him. Devil, you're a liar. Now, Lord, You take control of this, my brother in Christ." I had to make a declaration over my husband's life and let the enemy know that I know God was in control. Immediately the monitor began waving again. What a mighty God we serve! As the base hospital transported us to Wayne Memorial County Hospital, the doctors told us it was a true miracle that Robert was still alive. I just thanked God for His miracle. However, I did walk in my faith in Him and strongly believed that it was not time for Robert to go yet! God had promised me he would be saved someday.

The hospital drained black nicotine tar from Robert's body, which was clearly visible to see in his hospital room. Both lungs were filled with fluid, which caused him to have a pulmonary edema. After the Lord blessed him with more life, Robert gave up his forty-year smoking addiction. While in the hospital, he saw that his lungs were black and in horrible shape. He also received a clear picture of the tar they drained from his lungs. Both lungs were terribly damaged. Yes, prayers were answered seven years later! I just let Jesus Christ and His living Word change me totally that night! It just changed his life forever!

I truly thank God for allowing Robert to continue to live. I knew in my heart he was purposed for something greater and the Lord still had work for him to do. God is the God of second chances.

He makes things that are impossible possible through His great works (Mark 10:27). What was meant to be Robert's last day became the first day of seven more years before he dedicated his life to Christ! Our God is not only the loving God, but He's also very patient! God's anointing was for "such a time as this," so that my husband may live his best days ahead!

Watch this!

January 3, 1993, now, *my* life was 100 percent changed forever as well! I was truly born again, and my mind was renewed big time—stripping decades of my carnal-flesh self and even fifty years of soap box operas (I had watched the first episode of with my mother!) in the first TV in our neighborhood! It all had to go, even the worst chocolate addition you could ever see—and also with *football*, basketball, and baseball! It drove Robert batty, ridding all my hindrances! But *I was free* for a change—*down in my soul*! Hallelujah! Women of God (WOG), all I could do was keep living the life of Christ before him! *No*, it's not easy in the carnal flesh, especially with that loose James 3:5–8 *deadly tongue*! I could not let any false witnessing kill what God had begun for Robert ridding his past unto his best to come! Well, stay tuned!

You all, this is the Hebrews 9:16, 17 testator's testimony in force now! Amen. Of how Robert's eternal salvation truly got it's beginning in year 2000. Well, God knew how we mothers of the church sitting there on the pews at invitational time was truly going to be a blessing. I looked at 'these crutches coming down the Hallelujah avenue (isle)! My Robert came up to receive Jesus with more godly sorrow than we had ever seen in there! Hallelujah! He later told me that if I had run all around the church, like how I used to get my belief for praise over his mess, he would've gone back to his seat! Lord, have mercy! He was a serious man and never lied. Hallelujah! And his soul would've been lost into all eternity! Hallelujah! Saints, God sure did use our beautiful, loving, faithful, discerning mothers of the church that day to come to my aid! All I could do (all they let me do) was throw my hands up while sitting there and crying out, "Thank You, Lord, for Your great faithfulness! Thank You, Lord! Thank You, Lord!" It was Esther's scepter-touching anointed "such times" working at its best!

The Sweet "Mothers of St. Mark Church"Truly my life savers, & my husband Robert's eternal soul saver! Please read the account!

Watch this!

Robert now sure enough hears and reacts to the Lord's voice! He just was to me the used-to-be Bob no more. He called our blessed fortieth anniversary renewal in a proper church–sanctioned wedding with all the trimmings (on August 25, 2001)! It was a very, very, very special and sacrificing day for our pastor, General Bishop Alton A. Smith, on his fiftieth birthday. Also it was Robert's best man, Al Fitch's, birthday! Al was the brother Robert never had. Hallelujah! Just think how the pastor's entire family must have sacrificed also! So you reckon the pastor said as much (as he admired Mr. Bob, as the children he drove for thirteen blessed years on the Wayne County school bus called him); well, maybe the pastor just could not miss this very special day. The children just loved Mr. Bob's disciplining attitude and his wisdom of living it! He surely had a way with children! One year he was chosen as Bus Driver of the Year!

At the wedding, our children walked me down the aisle. I was given to Robert in hand by all, and we all lit the unity candle together! Many family from afar couldn't make it, but Robert just stole the show by overwhelming me with flying my beautiful longtime friend

Christine Ying in (from Kokomo, Indiana)! I hadn't seen her for over twenty years! He surprised me when he called her forward at the reception! You just know I was in another world!

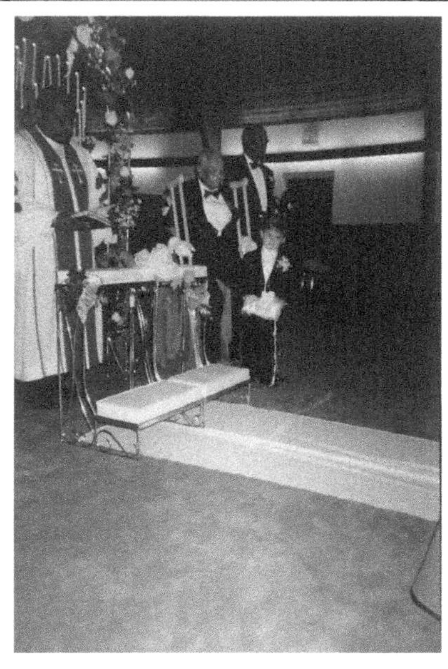

ROBERT & ESTHER'S 40TH ANNIVERSARY

8 25 '01

8 25 '01

Chief master sergeant Al & Pesrline Fitch, at their August 31, 2002 wedding!

But I don't know what I would've done without my longtime best North Carolina friends I ever had in this world! Matrons of honor were Ann Knight-Keller, with her uplifting belief and standing (on Philippians 4:6: "Be anxious for nothing!"), and Brenda Wooten, with her uplifting standing on such faithful promises as "Because He is, I am!" And there was my beautiful "tried and true" sweet sister Norma Elaine Goudy, who stood in place of my deceased mother she looked just like her! Hallelujah! The vocalists were Percy Royall III and our daughter Mary. Our daughter Margaret did the "Purpose." Her daughter Samantha and Tashia Cox were the flower girls, and little Ryan Carpenter was the ring bearer. And there was especially Jim and Nancy Moore, our blue-eyed soul brother and sister and earthly savior neighbors! Robert's best man was Al Fitch. Our lovely pastor's wife, Lady Doris Ann Smith, was the wedding directress, and the most marvelous decorators were Michael Ward and Barbara Vick. And there were many other attendants, groomsmen, and participants, etc. It was just a glorious day!

Robert with his friend cms. Alfred Fitch - the brother he never had!!! August 25 2001 -> Best man also!

To God be all the Glory, especially for His wedding theme for us (Revelations 19:9), "Called unto the Marriage Supper of the Lamb," which is about our Bridegroom (Jesus Christ), who cometh for His bride, the very church (Shushan's Esther was an exemplification!) "Hallelujah!"

All truly carried out this beautiful day for this modern day Esther's Perara family liken to Shu'-shan Esther's family of Jews, pulling together in corporate fasting, praying, believing with God's promises kept victoriously!

Ever so blessed on this highly successful peaceful day with the spiritual death of ole' spiritual Haman's evil protégé hindrances upon the Perara family to be anymore!

Praise God! As Robert and Esther were *joined to* the Lord by *one* (1 Corinthians 6:17) spirit, unto that *one*_(Ephesians 5:26, 27) glorious church, awaiting unto His one (Revelation 22:17) bride!

The marriage feast was such that it made all those who were called happy for accepting the invitation! In front of us was "The Table Hath Spread: Robert and Esther's Fortieth Year Feast of the Lord Is Going On and On and On!"

There was some powerful on-time prophesied manifestation *on the next day*, August 26, 2001! At my blessed initial sermon, while family and friends were still around, watch what really happened! This is the first time I've told anybody. May somebody out there be blessed with hope by it as well!

My "Precious Memory" treasurer forever!Robert and Esther - 1st time praying together, back from a military tour! His niece Sheila Graham could not resist taking picture!

That night, as I prayed for Any hinderant carnal flesh to cease from this Esther for the Holy Spirit to be all He needed to be from my instrumental body, it was as if His purposeful Living Word was being released to begin going on and on and on! It was not only in me but was as if the living water's spiritual working anointed power was flowing over time *into Robert and changing him*! It was as if his very (Matthew 5:6) hungry and thirsty soul was being fed, saying, "Jesus is mine!" And it was as if he was singing the song, "Heavenly Sunlight." Now that I see the light of *heavenly sunlight*, which is *flooding my soul with glory divine! Hallelujah!*

For after that blessed awesome season, Robert's life continued on, like the song does. *Hallelujah!* I *am rejoicing and singing His praises*. Jesus is mine!

Well, in the next year and four months, Robert proved it to many people who said, "What manner of man that has changed is *this*?" He was forgiving all that he needed to and asking the same, settling scores left and right. I was just touched! He had me pray for him and with him more than just the one or two times down on our knees! Bob and I prayed on our knees. I had to recall and recognize, reflecting back on August 25 and 26 of 2001, when I began seeing the harvest right before my eyes from the seeds I had sown (and others) in faithful prayers in the forty years in the wilderness of my mind! He came more and more nearer, believing God's (Genesis 12:3) blessed covenant with Abraham! With Robert receiving, *I am* also by faith believing in the blessing of Abraham with my spiritual inheritance! It's mine, it's mine, it's mine! And he soon entered into it eternally!

Is not this inheritance conducive to that of the blessing given to Uncle Mordecai (Esther 1:1–3) as a reward from King Ahasuerus in declaration of greatness for what he and Esther accomplished? These rewarded blessings of being accepted by the multitude of his brethren, being able to seek the wealth of his people, and speaking peace to all of his, well, Robert found this amazing correlation in today's (Galatians 5:16, 22, 23) flesh-dying love, joy, *peace* of King Jesus Christ's Spirit, carrying him to his obedient *last* and unto our Lord's declared greatness unto him of eternal *best* peaceful rest! It was for his patriarch witness that affected us in our spiritual Purim-Perara family celebration of what Jesus Christ has done for us down throughout all generations! He said He'll never leave nor forsake us! (Hebrews 13:5).

I must say, on the day of Robert's Home going celebration did we receive a marvelous show of his long time furtherance in keeping this kind of useful generations legacy moving! family pictures and relationship beginnings! He would 've been pleased!

Robert always teased that I married him for his most unusual name (which is a mixture of Spanish, Portuguese, French, and black American)! Nonetheless, I would ponder lots, repeating and thinking, "*There is something* in this name!" It was before I came to truly know love and latched on to *the one and only name* that means just *everything* to me—that's *Jesus Christ* (Philippians 2:9–11)!

Anyway, I found myself up in Spanish class in ministry school, and it was the Lord's sovereign will! Though I cannot speak a lick of Spanish (not using it daily), check this out! *I do* remember and *shall always* remember what Robert and others teased me at what my name means! *E*sther *Pera*ra is *espera—es, pera, espera*!

It means *expect, hope,* and *wait.* Hallelujah! It's the revealed predestined of my life! I've always had to humbly be patient and just wait. I find myself letting others—just everybody—go before me, not minding to be last. It's all God's (Psalms 24; Psalms 31:15).

Oh my god, saints! Now *the Lord* says this one, *I* didn't! The *last* shall be *first* (Matthew 20:16). Just a thought on this wise from the Lord! Chapter 3 "Chosen Feelings" of Robert and Esther's similarities are actually rightly so! In that, Robert put his old-fashioned self last in many ways! "Truth be told," Pastor Smith said, "lacking lots of things other men just normally thrived on." Like I told you all before, Robert was always assuring his family of being a good provider for us all. It confirms now why the Lord gave me this topic of this chapter!

It reminds you of the *best* of the goodies at the bottom of anything, like the strawberries that sink to the bottom in my milk shake! It's like the *last* savored-up piece of pie that your children ask you for. (Mothers just naturally feel more willing in this type of reserved sacrifice!) Look at how our child will ask us for that *last* lick of ice cream! I find myself so gratefully and satisfyingly giving up seats, spots, positions, decisions, arguments, disagreements, but oh, the Lord God *does* give me the go-ahead still in His Holy Spirit of Christ to lead, guide, and direct. You see, *He's* just a mighty force to be reckoned with! You see, this is our Esther spirit's set time with the Holy Ghost's boldness for scepter touching anointed such times of the Lord! You see, He's got to use *somebody for His glory*! Amen. Does He not say in Hebrews 13:5B that He shall *never* leave nor forsake us (His anointed presence)?

Well, the Lord came to call on Robert! As he heard the drummer's beat closer and closer and the one clear call for him—the bell—on Tuesday, December 11, 2002, at a ripe, blessed (Psalms 90:10) ole age of seventy!

On the way out of the door to work, I could not find my keys. I heard a hard thump on the bedroom floor. Robert was wedged so tightly between the bed and the wall! He was still with ole Haman's evil protégé spirit, having lost his last edged gallows on him already! With Robert's best victory in just Jesus, his Savior forever, the good Lord hurried me into the bedroom just in time before he took his last breath to be able to hear me say, "I love you, honey!" I know he heard me. Hallelujah! They were the best words that I ever could say to him, especially at his last.

I had an extreme sold-out change to Jesus Christ that was greatly needed in my silent, unconditional, loving (2 Corinthians 5:7) faith walk around Robert, upheld by God's promises alone! That's Esther's anointed such times with the needed touching of God's scepter at its best!

We each are different in this world, but as for me, I was free! I'm no longer bound, and there are no chains holding me. God was cleaning our house physically and spiritually and allowing the last *of our various trials to be seen as scripture* in the Spirit as being for Esther's anointed times. Nehemiah 8:10 says, "Joy of the Lord is my every bit of anointed strength needed. It was a trial for me that Robert was no longer with me and the children,. In my heart, I was joyful in knowing that he was with Jesus in our privileged touching of the spiritual scepter of God.

At this Robert's "last" and "best," it comes to my mind the conduciveness to year 2000 when he gave his life to Christ Jesus within, as if he was thinking of this song, "Just as I am, without one plea, but that Thy blood was shed for me, and that Thou biddest me, come to thee. To be 'absent from the body is to be Present with the Lord'" (2 Corinthians 5:8). Like Robert, our last days can be our best days also. It is up to us! God's master plan is for Robert to spend an eternal life with Him.

It's more than how you live till your last! But it's how your last continues on to be your eternal best! Hallelujah! The last lovely hands working on him in the Holy Spirit were of the late undertaker apostle Donnie L. McIntyre, his wife (Diane), and elite ministry staff. They put Robert's body into beautiful repose, unto the loving, awesome, eternal uppertaker's hands in keeping of his saved soul! We Perara family continue believing the blessed promises for ourselves as that for Robert's earthly decaying body, at Christ's return to become glorified to live with Him forevermore!

We are ever mindful of when Christ comes for us also; we too should be ready!

Therefore,
Farewell, sweet prince,
King and priest of your Perara family.
We'll see you in the morning.
Lord, you saved the best for last!

Acknowledgments

I am deeply grateful for the many influential people in my life. You have helped me turn my dreams of writing my book into a reality.

I truly thank the Lord for the following people and their most inspiring scriptures unto me: my late pastor, Bishop James L. Melvin, and his wife, Lady Mother Ada K. (Genesis 49:10); my beautiful pastor and mentor, General Bishop Alton A. Smith, and lovely wife, Lady Doris B. (Psalms 90:1; Acts 17:26); General Vice Bishop Malcolm S. Johnson and his wife, Lady Judy (Revelation 1:18); Bishop William J. Barber II and his wife, Rebecca (Matthew 25).

I thank the following Apostles: Norbert Simmons and his wife, Gwendolyn (Mark 11:24); Ivan T. Davis and his wife, Cheryl (2 Corinthians 1:20); the late Donnie McIntyre and his wife, Diane (Philippians 1:6); the late Dennis Jacobs and his wife, Ravonda (John 8:32); Bishop Chester L. Aycock and his late wife, Lady Dorothy, and his present wife, my spiritual daughter, Lady Tina (Psalms 121); Vice Bishop Richard M. Johnson and his wife, Lady Faye (Joshua 24:15) of the Goldsboro-Raleigh District Assembly Disciple Institute, along with its highly acclaimed professors and staff.

A very special appreciation for the auspices of General Assembly of the Churches of Christ, Disciples of Christ International, former presiding prelate General Bishop MacDonald Moses and his lovely wife, Evangelist Lady Carol (John 8:31).

Many special thanks to Barbara Short, Beverly Nadine Greene Durham, Emmanuel Holloman, Shelby Lofton, CMSgt (ret.) Alfred and Pearline Fitch, Ann K. Keller, and the late Luther Jones.

I thank the following special mentors: the Bishops Anthony Slater, William Phillips, Corletta Vaughn; Dr. Dwight Cannon; Dr. Alma F. Jenkins, the late Dr. Kizzie Core; Dr. Dorothy Best; the pastors Mary Brown, Dorothy Heath, Evelena Oliver, Rev. Evelyn

Gettis-Lee, Dianna Peppers, Naomi Williams, Bajei Garrett, and Janice Brown-Vick.

I thank the following special encouragers: St. Mark Church associate ministers, deacons, trustees, and mother board, especially Mary Higginbotham, Bert Davis, Shirley Edwards, Lady Cassandra Stevenson, Hattie Harris, Martha Smith, Constance Coram, Alma Jean Taylor, Betty Johnson, Iris Durham, Shirley C. Howard, Elder Keith Anderson, Sara Brewington, James and Nancy Moore, Brenda Wooten, and Glenda Wiggins, Lawrence Durham, Jimmie Ford and Patricia Burden, Dr. Billy Newton.

I thank the Special Families: Langston; Shealy; McNair; Grantham; Chesnutt; Hood; Christine Ying-House; Avey and Lamb (West Virginia family); my late parents, George and Margaret Grady; my children; my late brother Robert and his wife, Shirley Grady; my sister Norma Elaine Goudy and her late husband, Derrick; my late praying grandmothers, Esther Tompkins and Emma Grady, and their husbands; my cousin Billy Grady; chaplains: the late Reverend Hubert R. Hunting and family, Major Josephine Pinkney and Darius; and my late Uncle Bill Grady (my Mordecai), who raised me spiritually in my later teenage and young adult years!

I am forever grateful for the Spirit-filled hands of the late undertaker, Apostle Donnie L. McIntyre, his wife (Diane), and the elite ministry staff for the final repose of my husband, Robert, unto our Great Uppertaker's Hands!

Last but not the least, I will always be eternally grateful to the staff at Seymour Johnson AFB and at Wayne Memorial Hospital of Goldsboro, North Carolina, especially Dr. Christene Illunga, Dr. David Rockwell, and Robert's private nurse, Harriet Harris!

Note to the Readers

Throughout the entire book, all scriptures were taken from the New King James Version Open Bible by Thomas Nelson Publishers, copyright 1997 by Thomas Nelson Inc.

All the words that are accompanied by definitions were taken from *Webster's New World College Dictionary* (3rd edition) by McMillian General Reference, copyright 1997 by Simon and Schuster Inc.

About the Author

Evangelist Esther E. Perara, who has spilled her heart out and emptied her soul, is such an unselfish, unconditional loving, caring sister unto all of God's people!

She was just a timid little ole country girl hailing from Kokomo, Indiana, with such a humble and determined calling on her discovered unusual life. God's purpose unfolded in her later trying, most challenging, yet faithful years!

She is motherless and fatherless in such needy years yet so blessed with such a beautiful shining-armor example of mentoring, lovely overseeing, and God-given help from the Lord—as any young girl would ever need in her vulnerable predestined life—in her Uncle Bill (her Mordecai), Deacon William H. Grady.

Now, without a shadow of a doubt, she does know what "to God be all the glory" truly means! You see, just as the Father (God) purposed His very own Son, Jesus, to ultimately suffer on the cross of Calvary to free His great multitude of people, it wore her up (in hopes of reaching just one) in great evangelistic commission (Matthew 28:18–20) through oneness and resolve.

To not think it so strange (1 Peter 4:12).

His predestined calling on her life is this: to be used for His glory.

Esther is anointed for such times, touching the scepter of God!

Thus, this is the reason He has given her as to why His Name (God) is not seen physically in the book of Esther in the Bible; it's for each of us to see Him spiritually for our own accountable selves—in Jesus's Name!

Evangelist Esther Perara

PO Box 11503

Goldsboro, NC 27532

919-344-6790

eeppraises414@att.net gmail.com

CPSIA information can be obtained
at www.ICGtesting.com
Printed in the USA
FFHW021600180119
50206771-55174FF